BOWLS!

b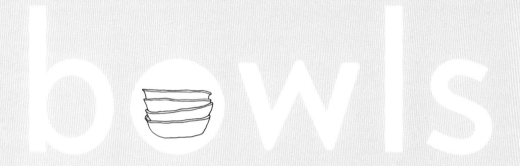wls!

Recipes and Inspirations for Healthful One-Dish Meals

Molly Watson

Photographs by
Nicole Franzen

CHRONICLE BOOKS

SAN FRANCISCO

Library of Congress Cataloging-in-Publication
Data available.

ISBN 978-1-4521-5619-4

Manufactured in China

Designed by Vanessa Dina
Illustrations by Rachel Harrell
Prop styling by Kira Corbin
Food styling by Lillian Kang
Typesetting by Frank Brayton

Chronicle books and gifts are available at special
quantity discounts to corporations, professional associations, literacy programs, and other
organizations. For details and discount information, please contact our premiums department
at corporatesales@chroniclebooks.com or at
1-800-759-0190.

10 9 8 7 6 5 4 3 2

Chronicle Books LLC
680 Second Street
San Francisco, California 94107
www.chroniclebooks.com

They are the first to go. The cupboard still holds a tall stack of plates, but the bowls are gone. They are filling the dishwasher, sitting in the sink, or drying on the rack. Well before bowls were in fashion in the food world, we were eating out of them at a furious pace in my house.

We loaded them up with soup and cereal and stew. Snacks of popcorn. Garnish-laden salads. And we used them first because my favorite breakfasts and lunches have long been leftovers from dinner, heated up, plopped in a bowl, and topped with cheese or hot sauce or a dollop of sour cream or a handful of arugula—a final fresh addition to give the leftovers new life.

In short, bowls represent everything you want in a meal: easy to make, tasty to eat, and, more often than not, wonderfully frugal. Best of all, they're flexible (always flexible!). Add or subtract elements to suit your individual taste—and that of everyone at the table.

Bowls are perfect for weeknight eating, particularly on those evenings when a stop at the store for something specific isn't in the cards. Often as not, you can assemble a delicious bowl from what's hiding in the cupboard or sitting in the fridge. If you have your favorite condiments on hand, they do magic in bringing otherwise disparate foods together.

Case in point: One night while writing up recipes for this book, I took some leftover rice, mixed it with a can of tuna, drizzled on a little chile oil, threw in a handful of chopped celery, and scattered arugula on top. Was it the best bowl I've ever eaten? I can't say that it was. Would I purposefully make it again? Um, probably not. Was it a tasty and serviceable dinner made from things I found in the kitchen, ready in three minutes, and relatively healthful? Yes it was.

Up ahead you'll find Part 1, which contains easy recipes for creating simple components. Part 2 provides some appealing combinations that serve as templates or inspiration for throwing those components together into satisfying bowl-based meals.

Watch out, though. Once you get used to bowl-centric eating, you may find yourself turning to this irresistible tableware even when you have time to cook an elaborate supper from scratch. That's where Part 3 comes in. It is a culinary goldmine packed with complete, sometimes complex creations.

Whether you turn to a simple lineup of rice, spinach, and eggs or a more elaborate combination, may your bowls be well used.

A NOTE ON SUBSTITUTIONS
Bowls are flexible. Full stop.

A good rule of thumb: if you come across a combination or a recipe for a bowl that sounds good except for one element, it's best to substitute like with like. Replace a grain with a grain, meat with meat, cooked vegetable with cooked vegetable, crunchy garnish with crunchy garnish, and so on.

That said, even that constraint may rein too tight. Some of the suggestions in these pages are classic combinations put together in a new bowl-centric way. Ethiopian fasting foods (often served as "veggie combos") are thrown in the air to come down transformed in the Addis Ababa Lane Bowl. Chicken paprikash and other Hungarian flavors find themselves piled together in the Budapest Bowl.

Others, however, may well read like random mishmashes. They are and they aren't. They are random, but the jumbled nature of bowls is exactly where their charm and power lie.

So go forth, put things randomly in bowls, top them with something fresh and tasty, and dig in!

A NOTE ON AMOUNTS
The recipes in this book are for four modest servings, and the yield of any subrecipe assumes the food will be combined with other things in a bowl (or on a plate, if that's how you roll). Increase or decrease amounts according to who's tucking into the bowls around your table.

ABOUT THE ORDER OF OPERATIONS
In Part 3, several components are being prepared for each bowl, so I have provided an Order of Operations with each recipe that outlines a plan of attack. Sometimes a recipe can be hurried along by skipping among the elements, such as preparing vegetables and sauces while grains or meats cook. In all cases, the Order of Operations quickly points out the most efficient way to get everything chopped, cooked, and ready to assemble.

bowl basics

Building Blocks of a Tasty Bowl

The best bowls have at least one of each of the following elements. That said, feel free to skip one (or two) or use more than one from any given category. Bowls are all about flexibility and personal taste, so do as your taste buds—and the contents of your refrigerator and your cupboards—dictate to create bowls that range from simply healthful to over-the-top indulgent.

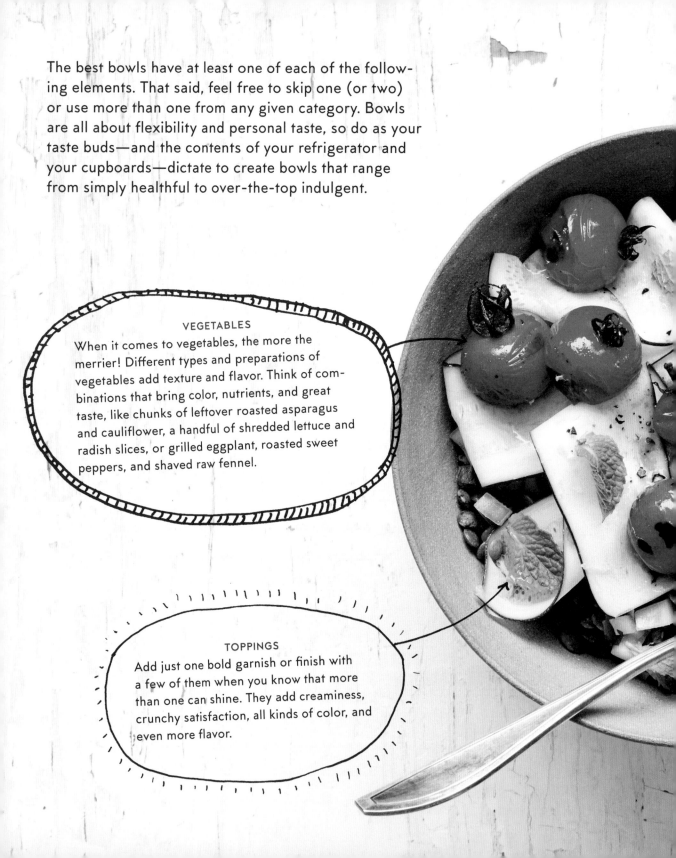

VEGETABLES

When it comes to vegetables, the more the merrier! Different types and preparations of vegetables add texture and flavor. Think of combinations that bring color, nutrients, and great taste, like chunks of leftover roasted asparagus and cauliflower, a handful of shredded lettuce and radish slices, or grilled eggplant, roasted sweet peppers, and shaved raw fennel.

TOPPINGS

Add just one bold garnish or finish with a few of them when you know that more than one can shine. They add creaminess, crunchy satisfaction, all kinds of color, and even more flavor.

SAUCE
Condiments, dressings, and sauces of all kinds, whether store-bought or homemade, deliver a hit of flavor and bring together all of the elements in the bowl.

PROTEIN
The protein can be any one of the usual suspects: meat, fish, poultry, tofu, beans, or even just an egg plopped on top. Nothing says you have to add a protein-centric food, but to give a bowl the satisfying heft of a meal, it sure does help.

BASE
Bases are foods that tend to fill you up and soak up flavors from the rest of the ingredients in the bowl. A huge range of options is possible, including grains, legumes of all sorts, and vegetables.

That's the bowls concept. Use the following basic recipes with this blueprint in mind, jump ahead to Part 2 for some easy-to-pull-together combinations, or dive in deep with the more involved composed-bowl recipes in Part 3.

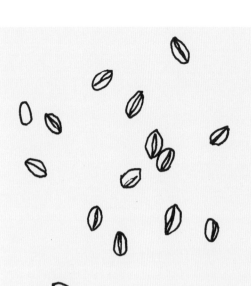

GRAINS & THE LIKE

The most common bases for bowls are rice and quinoa, and multiple ways to cook both of them are included here. You'll find other grains, pseudograins, and noodles here, as well. There is no need to stick to grains as the bases for your bowls, though. Beans and other legumes of all sorts can play that role, too, as can mashed, roasted, or hashed vegetables.

As noted earlier, these recipes yield modest servings for four. You can easily adjust the amounts for larger batches and store the extra for another meal or two. Making a large batch of grains and freezing meal-size portions is a great way to work longer-cooking whole grains into everyday meals.

Barley

3 cups [720 ml] water or broth
1 cup [200 g] pearled barley
½ tsp salt (if using water)

In a medium saucepan over high heat, bring the water or broth to a boil. Add the barley and the salt if using water, bring back to a boil, adjust the heat to maintain a steady simmer, and cook, stirring frequently, until the barley is tender, 25 to 30 minutes. If any liquid remains, drain it off. Use immediately, or spread on a baking sheet to cool, then transfer to an airtight container and refrigerate for up to 3 days or freeze for up to 6 months.

Most barley sold in the United States is pearled, which means both the outer hull and some or all of the bran has been removed. The term *pearled* refers to the polishing or "pearling" of the grain to remove the bran. Whole-grain barley, sometimes known as hulled barley, has had only the toughest outer hull removed, with the bran left intact. If you are using whole-grain barley, you will need to increase the cooking time to close to 1 hour and add extra liquid as needed for the barley to become tender.

Mushroom Barley Pilaf (page 121)
Swiss Chard–Barley Pilaf (page 104)

Brown Rice
(Long Grain, Medium Grain, Short Grain, or Sweet)

2 cups [480 ml] water or broth
1 cup [200 g] rice
½ tsp salt (if using water)

In a medium saucepan over high heat, combine the water or broth, rice, and the salt if using water. Bring to a boil, stir once, cover, turn the heat to low, and cook, undisturbed, for 45 minutes. Remove from the heat—leave the lid on!—and let sit for 10 to 15 minutes. The grains will be tender and the liquid will be absorbed. Fluff with a fork and serve, or let cool, transfer to an airtight container, and refrigerate for up to 3 days or freeze for up to 6 months.

I go out of my way to keep sweet brown rice—aka sticky brown rice—in my cupboard (it's not always easy to find; health food stores and co-ops are often the best bet for tracking it down). It has the same short, plump kernels as sticky white rice, also known as glutinous rice or sweet rice, and cooks up the same way, but it has all of the fiber and nutrients of regular brown rice. Its texture is great in saucy bowls, and I find it pleases most eaters who are not otherwise thrilled with finding brown rice on the menu.

Gingered Coconut Brown Rice (page 93)
Sesame Brown Rice (page 133)
Taqueria-Style Rice (page 89)

Buckwheat

1 cup [170 g] buckwheat
2 cups [480 ml] water
½ tsp salt

Heat a large frying pan over medium-high heat. When the pan is hot, add the buckwheat and cook, stirring, until browned and toasted, about 5 minutes (skip this step if starting with toasted buckwheat). Add the water and salt and bring to a simmer. Cover, turn the heat to low, and cook until the buckwheat is tender, 15 to 20 minutes. Remove the lid and simmer to cook off any remaining liquid, if necessary. Use immediately, or spread on a baking sheet to cool, then transfer to an airtight container and refrigerate for up to 3 days or freeze for up to 6 months.

Buckwheat is a whole grain (actually a whole psuedograin, since it is botanically a seed) from which only the tough outer hull has been removed. It is sold as is or as roasted (or toasted) kernels, sometimes labeled "buckwheat groats" or "kasha." The term *kasha* is also applied to cooked toasted buckwheat, which can be prepared plain or as described on page 84.

Bulgur

1 cup [140 g] bulgur
¼ tsp salt
2 cups [480 ml] boiling water

In a medium heatproof bowl, combine the bulgur and salt. Add the water, cover, and let sit until the bulgur is tender and the water is absorbed, about 20 minutes. (Sometimes a batch absorbs less liquid; if the bulgur is tender, drain off any excess water.) Use immediately, or spread on a baking sheet to cool, then transfer to an airtight container and refrigerate for up to 3 days or freeze for up to 6 months.

Some cooks confuse bulgur and cracked wheat. Bulgur is whole wheat berries that have been steamed or parboiled, dried, and then cracked. It is sold in fine, medium, and coarse grinds. Cracked wheat, which is more difficult to find, is whole wheat berries that are cracked with no preliminary processing. (To confuse the cook even more, some packages containing bulgur are labeled "cracked wheat bulgur.") If you opt for cracked wheat over bulgur, you will need to cook it like Freekeh (page 17).

Browned Garlic Bulgur (page 149)
Seeded Bulgur Pilaf (page 91)

Farro

1 cup [180 g] semipearled farro

Bring a pot of salted water to a boil. Add the farro, adjust the heat to maintain a steady simmer, and cook until the farro is tender to the bite, about 20 minutes. Drain and use immediately, or spread on a baking sheet to cool, then transfer to an airtight container and refrigerate for up to 3 days or freeze for up to 6 months.

Farro is sold in three forms: whole grain, semipearled (*semipearlato*), and pearled (*perlato*). The inedible hull has been removed from the whole grain, the hull and part of the bran from the semipearled, and the hull and all of the bran from the pearled. The instructions provided here are for semipearled farro, which takes less time to cook than the more nutritious whole grain, but which has more nutrients than pearled farro.

Nutted Farro (page 115)

Freekeh

1 cup [180 g] freekeh
2 cups [480 ml] water
½ tsp salt

Heat a medium or large, heavy saucepan over medium-high heat. When the pan is hot, add the freekeh and cook, stirring or shaking the pan often, until the freekeh is toasted and fragrant, about 3 minutes. Add the water and salt and bring to a boil. Cover, turn the heat to low, and cook, undisturbed, until the liquid is absorbed and the freekeh is tender, 20 to 25 minutes. Remove from the heat, uncover, fluff with a fork, re-cover, and let sit for 10 minutes before fluffing again and serving. Or spread on a baking sheet to cool, then transfer to an airtight container, and refrigerate for up to 3 days or freeze for up to 6 months.

Rich in fiber and protein, freekeh is young green wheat kernels that have been roasted and then cracked. A nutritious whole grain, it has long been popular in some Middle Eastern cuisines. It is not as storage-friendly as many other grains, however, and I've come across many packages that have turned rancid. But if you luck into fresh freekeh, it brings a great nutty, slightly smoky flavor to a bowl.

Lemony Freekeh (page 143)

Polenta

4 cups [960 ml] water or broth
½ tsp salt (if using water)
1 cup [140 g] polenta

In a medium saucepan over high heat, bring the water or broth to a boil. Add the salt if using water, then as the liquid bubbles, add the polenta while whisking continuously. Adjust the heat to maintain a simmer and cook, stirring with a wooden spoon to keep the polenta from sticking to the bottom of the pan, until a thick porridge forms. It will be ready to eat in 20 to 25 minutes. For a deeper flavor, cook the polenta for 30 to 40 minutes, but be sure to continue to scrape the polenta from the bottom of the pan as you stir. Or, you can be less traditional with pretty much the same results: after whisking in the polenta, turn the heat to low, cover, and stir every 5 to 10 minutes until thickened, 20 to 40 minutes total. Use immediately or transfer to an airtight container, let cool, cover, and refrigerate for up to 3 days.

Quinoa

1 cup [180 g] quinoa (see note)
2 cups [480 ml] water or broth
¼ tsp salt (if using water)

Quinoa must be rinsed or toasted before cooking to temper its bitterness.

TO RINSE: Pour the quinoa into a fine-mesh sieve and agitate vigorously under cool running water for a minute or two. In a medium saucepan over high heat, bring the water or broth to a boil. Add the quinoa and the salt if using water, cover, turn the heat to low, and cook, undisturbed, until the quinoa is tender and fluffy and the liquid is absorbed, about 20 minutes.

TO TOAST: Place a large frying pan over medium-high heat. When the pan is hot, add the quinoa and cook, stirring frequently, until toasted and fragrant, about 3 minutes. Add the water or broth and the salt if using water and bring to a simmer, cover, turn the heat to low, and cook, undisturbed, until the quinoa is tender and fluffy and the liquid is absorbed, about 20 minutes.

Use the quinoa immediately, or spread on a baking sheet to cool, then transfer to an airtight container and refrigerate for up to 3 days or freeze for up to 6 months.

Three kinds of quinoa are available: white, which is the most common; red; and the much rarer black. All three can be cooked this way, with the red quinoa typically taking a few minutes longer than the white and the black a little longer than the red. All three types have a natural coating called saponin that gives the grain a bitter flavor. Even though some commercial quinoa is sold "pre-rinsed," I advise you to treat any quinoa you buy just in case, either by rinsing it or toasting it before cooking. Both methods are included here and work equally well.

Rye

1 cup [200 g] rye kernels
4 cups [960 ml] water
2 tsp salt (optional)

Put the rye in a medium saucepan, pour in the water, and add the salt, if using. Place over high heat, bring to a boil, lower the heat to maintain a gentle simmer, and cook, adding more water as needed to keep the rye covered, until the kernels are tender to the bite, about 45 minutes. The rye will never turn truly soft, just chewable. Pour into a fine-mesh sieve to drain well. Use immediately, or spread on a baking sheet to cool, then transfer to an airtight container and refrigerate for up to 3 days or freeze for up to 6 months.

Whole rye kernels, or berries, can be difficult to find, and once you do track them down, they take a while to cook. But you will be happy you made the search and took the time in the kitchen, as they are remarkably toothsome and do not have as intense a rye flavor as you might expect.

Soba Noodles

12 oz [340 g] dried soba noodles

Bring a pot of salted water to a boil. Add the noodles and cook according to package instructions (timing can vary greatly depending on the brand); they should be tender to the bite. Be careful not to overcook, as they can turn to mush alarmingly fast. Drain into a colander and rinse well under cool running water, or they will clump together in a most unappealing fashion. Use immediately, or transfer to an airtight container and refrigerate for up to 3 days.

A classic of the Japanese kitchen, soba noodles are made from buckwheat flour (sometimes combined with wheat flour) and are traditionally served both hot and cold. They make a great base because they readily soak up the flavors of other ingredients and contribute a nutty, earthy taste to the bowl.

Steel-Cut Oats

3 to 4 cups [720 to 960 ml] water
1 cup [160 g] steel-cut oats
¼ tsp salt

In a medium saucepan over high heat, bring the water to a boil, using the smaller amount of water if you want the oats to remain intact and chewier and the larger amount if you want porridge-like oats. Add the oats and salt, stir, and bring back to a boil. Lower the heat to keep the oats at a steady simmer and cook, stirring now and again, until the oats are tender, 20 to

CONT'D

30 minutes. Use immediately, or transfer to an airtight container, let cool, cover, and refrigerate for up to 3 days or freeze for up to 6 months.

VARIATION

For a greater depth of flavor, melt 1 Tbsp butter in the saucepan. Add the oats and cook, stirring, until fragrant and toasted, about 3 minutes. Add the water and salt, bring to a boil, and cook as directed.

Steel-cut oats have a heartier texture than old-fashioned rolled oats, which makes them my choice for my everyday bowl of breakfast oatmeal. But they are a tasty option for savory supper bowls, too. If you happen to come upon whole oats, they stand in nicely for barley, farro, or rye; cook them in boiling water until tender and then drain, as for the other grains.

White Rice

(Long Grain, Medium Grain, or Short Grain)

2 cups [480 ml] water
1 cup [200 g] white rice
¼ tsp salt

In a medium saucepan over high heat, bring the water to a boil. Add the rice and salt, cover, turn the heat to low, and cook, undisturbed, for 15 minutes. Remove the pan from the heat and let sit—leave the lid on!—for another 5 minutes. The grains will be tender and the liquid will be absorbed. Fluff with a fork and serve, or spread on a baking sheet to cool, then transfer to an airtight container and refrigerate for up to 3 days or freeze for up to 6 months.

Wild Rice

1 cup [180 g] wild rice
¼ tsp salt (if steaming)
3 cups [720 ml] water (if steaming)

You can either boil or steam the rice.

TO BOIL: Bring a large pot of salted water to a boil over high heat. Add the wild rice and cook until tender. The timing will vary depending on the age of the rice. Start testing at 30 minutes, but it will likely take at least 45 minutes. Drain the rice.

TO STEAM: In a medium saucepan over high heat, combine the wild rice, salt, and water and bring to a boil. Cover, lower the heat to maintain a steady simmer, and cook until the rice is tender and the kernels pop open, 45 to 60 minutes. Uncover the rice and fluff it with a fork. If necessary, simmer, stirring occasionally, to cook off any excess liquid, 5 to 10 minutes longer.

Use immediately, or transfer to an airtight container, let cool, cover, and refrigerate for up to 3 days or freeze for up to 6 months.

If you decide to boil the rice, the kernels will be intact and tender but slightly firm. If you opt to steam the rice, the kernels will "pop" open and be softer.

Wild Rice Black Lentil Pilaf (page 129)

BEANS & LENTILS

Legumes, such as black beans, chickpeas, split peas, and lentils, add fiber, nutrients, flavor, and bulk to bowls. They work both as bases and, in smaller portions, on grain or vegetable bases. Canned beans are a quick and easy way to a filling bowl, and I turn to them fairly often. Always rinse them thoroughly, however, as the canned liquid can really gum things up. But I also cook up big batches of dried beans and then freeze the cooked beans, immersed in their cooking liquid, in portions that I can grab and thaw easily. This gives me the convenience of canned beans but with the superior flavor and texture of beans cooked from scratch. Lentils and split peas are a way to get freshly cooked legumes ready in not too much time.

Lentils

1 cup [200 g] lentils, rinsed
3 cups [720 ml] water
1 onion, halved (optional)
2 garlic cloves (optional)
1 bay leaf (optional)
Salt

In a medium pot over high heat, combine the lentils and water and bring to a boil. Add the onion, garlic, and/or a bay leaf (if using). Lower the heat to maintain a lively simmer, cover partially, and cook, stirring now and again and adding more water if necessary, to keep the lentils covered, until tender, about 15 minutes for tiny black lentils and up to 30 minutes for large brown lentils. Remove from the heat, add salt to the water until it tastes salty, let sit for 5 minutes, drain, and discard the onion, garlic, and/or bay leaf if used. Alternatively, remove from the heat, drain the lentils, discard the onion, garlic, and/or bay leaf if used, and season with salt.

Use immediately, or let cool, transfer to an airtight container, and refrigerate for up to 1 week or freeze for up to 6 months.

Brown, green (including the prized French Puy variety), and black (often labeled "beluga" because of their resemblance to caviar) lentils all cook up fairly quickly, making them perfect for adding to bowls on a weeknight. Like many beans and grains, lentils can also be cooked in large batches and then refrigerated or frozen. Yellow, white, and red lentils are almost always sold hulled, and because they don't have skins, their cooking

time is shorter. They also tend to turn mushy in the blink of an eye, so it is best to use them in soups or in grain and/or vegetable mixtures for adding to bowls.

Herbed Lentils (page 81)
Red Lentil Quinoa Pilaf (page 96)
Wild Rice Black Lentil Pilaf (page 129)

Basic Dried Beans

1 lb [455 g] dried beans, rinsed and soaked (see note)
Salt

Drain the beans, put in a large pot, and cover with fresh water. Bring to a boil over high heat and skim off and discard any foam from the surface. Lower the heat to maintain a steady simmer and cook the beans until they are about three-quarters done. They should be slightly firm and smell like cooked beans. Add enough salt to make the water taste salty and continue to simmer until just done. They should be tender to the bite but not mushy. The overall timing will depend on the type and age of the beans.

To use some of the beans immediately, drain the needed portion. To store the beans, divide them among airtight containers, cover with their cooking liquid, and refrigerate for up to 1 week or freeze for up to 6 months.

Whether you have chickpeas, white beans, kidney beans, black beans, cranberry beans—you get the idea—all dried beans are cooked the same way. They will cook up most evenly if you put them in a bowl, cover them generously with water, and let them soak overnight. You can also quick soak the beans: put them in a pot, add water to cover, bring to a boil, cover the pot, and let sit off the heat for 1 hour. The fresher your stash of dried beans, the less soaking time they will require before cooking and the less time they will take to cook. Most dried beans will be ready in 25 to 45 minutes.

Because dried beans must be soaked, take a relatively long time to cook, and freeze well, the yield here is greater than for other recipes, roughly eight servings rather than four. To store the beans, divide them among airtight containers, cover with their cooking liquid, and refrigerate for up to 1 week or freeze for up to 6 months.

Pot Likker Beans

1 Tbsp olive oil
1 onion, chopped
2 carrots, peeled and chopped
2 celery stalks, chopped
1 to 2 garlic cloves, finely chopped
1 lb [455 g] dried beans (any kind), rinsed and soaked (see Basic Dried Beans note, left)
1 bay leaf
Salt

In a large pot over medium-high heat, combine the olive oil, onion, carrot, celery, and garlic and cook, stirring occasionally, until the vegetables soften a bit, about 3 minutes. Drain the beans and add them to the pot along with the bay leaf. Add fresh water just to cover the beans and bring to a boil over high heat. Skim off any foam that forms on the surface, lower the heat to maintain a steady simmer, and cook, stirring now and again, until the beans are just barely tender to the bite. Stir in 1 tsp salt. Taste the liquid and add more salt if needed. Continue simmering until the beans are tender. The overall timing will depend on the type and age of the beans. Remove and discard the bay leaf.

Use some of the beans immediately (you may want to dole them out with a slotted spoon to keep the bowls from getting too liquidy). As with the other dried bean recipes, this one yields about eight servings. To store the beans, divide them among airtight containers, cover with their cooking liquid, and refrigerate for up to 1 week or freeze for up to 6 months.

Drunken Black Beans

2 Tbsp olive oil

2 onions, chopped

2 garlic cloves, finely chopped

Two 12-fl oz [360-ml] bottles beer

4 cups [960 ml] water

1 lb [455 g] black beans (aka turtle beans), rinsed and soaked (see Basic Dried Beans note, page 23)

Salt

In a large pot over medium-high heat, warm the olive oil. Add the onions and cook, stirring occasionally, until they are soft, about 3 minutes. Add the garlic and cook, stirring, until fragrant, about 1 minute. Pour in the beer and water, then drain the beans and add them to the pot. Raise the heat to high, bring to a boil, lower the heat to maintain a steady simmer, and skim off any foam that forms on the surface. Cook, stirring occasionally, until the beans are just tender, 30 to 40 minutes. Add enough salt to make the water taste a bit salty, then remove the pot from the heat and let sit until the beans are fully tender, 15 to 20 minutes.

Use some of the beans immediately (you may want to dole them out with a slotted spoon to keep the bowls from getting too liquidy). As with the other dried bean recipes, this one yields about eight servings. To store the beans, divide them among airtight containers, cover with their cooking liquid, and refrigerate for up to 1 week or freeze for up to 6 months.

Browned Onion Split Peas (page 84)

Cilantro Pinto Beans (page 89)

Dilled White Beans (page 121)

Falafel-esque Chickpeas (page 78)

Spiced Roasted Chickpeas (page 87)

Sautéed White Beans (page 112)

Soupy Chickpeas (page 91)

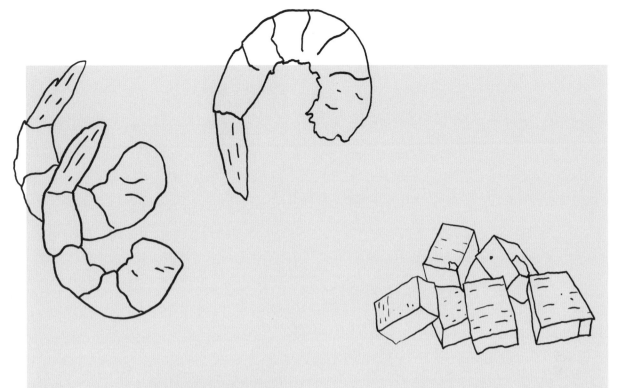

PROTEINS

Meat, fish, chicken, tofu, and other protein-heavy foods that shine when in bite-size pieces tend to work best in bowls. Sometimes proteins turn up whole too, of course, such as a fried egg or a few shrimp. Here are some simple ways to cook up these staples to give bowls appetite-satisfying power. Most of these recipes, as with most of the others in this part, yield four modest servings.

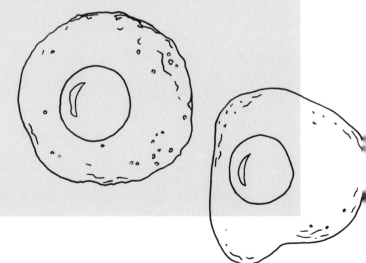

Eggs are perhaps the easiest way to turn a mishmash of things in a bowl into a meal. Somehow, no matter what crazy combination is underneath, topping a bowl with a poached, fried, or soft-boiled egg brings the whole thing together (or is that just the luscious yolk getting all over everything?).

Poached Eggs

2 Tbsp distilled white vinegar or fresh lemon juice per 1 cup [240 ml] water
4 eggs, at room temperature

Pour water to a depth of 2 in [5 cm] into a 10-in [25-cm] wide, shallow pan and add the vinegar (the acid will help the egg whites coagulate quickly, which in turn helps the eggs keep their shape while cooking). Place over medium-high heat and heat until bubbles are visible along the bottom and sides of the pan but don't break on, or come to, the surface. If you have an instant-read thermometer, use it to hit the magical 180°F [82°C]. Adjust the heat to maintain this temperature. Lay a clean kitchen towel or layered paper towels nearby for draining the eggs.

Crack each egg into its own ramekin or small measuring cup. (Cracking the eggs into individual vessels allows you to remove any bits of shell, start again if a yolk breaks, and have more control when guiding an egg into the pan.) If you have poaching rings, go ahead and put them in the pan. (Want do-it-yourself poaching rings? You can use cleaned tuna fish cans with both the top and bottom removed.)

One at a time, and working quickly, hold each ramekin right at the surface of the water and gently slip the egg into the water (or into a ring, if using). Carefully spoon a little of the poaching water over each egg to help set the top. For poached eggs with set whites and warm, runny yolks, cook for 2 minutes. For set yolks, cook for 2 minutes longer.

Using a slotted spoon, gently lift each egg out of the poaching liquid. If an egg has stuck a bit to the pan, carefully work the edge of the spoon between the egg and the pan to loosen the egg before lifting it out. Set the eggs on the kitchen towel or paper towels to drain off as much liquid as possible. Pat their tops dry, if you like, and transfer to the bowls.

A poached egg brings a softness—almost a juiciness—to a bowl. I've found that some people are intimidated by poaching in general. If you are among them, it is well worth getting over your reluctance for the many rewards poaching reaps.

Soft-Boiled Eggs

4 eggs

Bring a medium saucepan of water to a boil over high heat. (The water must be deep enough for the eggs to be completely submerged when they are added.) Using a slotted spoon, carefully lower the eggs, one at a time, into the boiling water, then adjust the heat to maintain a low boil or strong simmer.

Cook the eggs for 4 minutes for runny yolks and barely set whites, 5 minutes for runny yolks and set whites, 6 minutes for partially set yolks, or 7 minutes for soft-set yolks. Using the spoon, lift the eggs out of the water. Carefully peel each egg under cool running water, pat them dry, and add them to your bowls.

Hard-Boiled Eggs

4 eggs

To minimize the possibility of the eggs cracking while they cook, you can prick a teeny hole in the end of each egg with a tack, though it isn't necessary. Put the eggs in a pan large enough to hold them in a single layer without crowding. Add cool water to cover by 1 in [2.5 cm] and place over high heat. Bring to a boil (you want a real boil, with large bubbles coming up all over, rather than a simmer with a few bubbles along the edges). Cover the pan, turn off the heat, and let the eggs sit for *exactly* 14 minutes. Set a timer in case you get distracted.

While the eggs sit, prepare a large bowl of ice water. When the eggs are ready, drain them and transfer them to the ice water. To serve warm hard-boiled eggs, let them sit in the ice water just until you can handle them, then peel them. To serve them cold, leave them in the water until they are cool to the touch. You can then peel them and serve them, or you can refrigerate them unpeeled for up to 2 days before using.

For even easier-to-peel eggs, save the hot cooking water, and after the eggs cool down in their ice-water bath, dip them back into the hot water for 10 to 20 seconds. I also find peeling them under cool running water works well if you want to serve warm hard-boiled eggs. Be sure to pat them dry before transferring them to the bowls.

Fried Eggs

1 Tbsp olive or other cooking oil
4 eggs
¼ tsp salt (optional)

In a large frying pan over medium-high heat, warm the oil, swirling the pan to coat the bottom evenly. One at a time, crack the eggs and slip them into the hot pan. The pan is the correct temperature if the eggs bubble a bit when they hit the pan. Sprinkle with the salt, if you like, and cook, undisturbed, until the whites are set and the edges start to brown, about 2 minutes. Use a spatula to turn the eggs and cook on the other side for

CONT'D

about 30 seconds for over-easy eggs, 1 minute for over-medium eggs, and up to 2 minutes for fully cooked yolks. For sunny-side-up eggs, let the eggs cook without flipping until the whites are set and the yolks are done to your liking. Transfer the eggs directly to the bowls.

Scrambled Eggs

4 to 8 eggs
1 Tbsp water, milk, or heavy cream for each egg
1 to 2 Tbsp butter
¼ to ½ tsp salt

Crack the eggs into a medium bowl, add the water, and whisk until the eggs are well blended.

In a medium frying pan over medium heat, melt the butter, adjusting the amount according to how many eggs you are cooking. When the butter stops foaming, turn the heat to medium-low. Whisk the salt into the eggs, again adjusting the amount according to how many eggs you are cooking. Pour the eggs into the hot pan.

For firmer eggs with large curds, let the eggs sit and cook until the bottom and edges have begun to solidify, about 1 minute, then scrape and lift the edges of the cooked egg with a spatula and allow the uncooked portion to run underneath the lifted portion. Working around the edge of the pan, fold the cooked portions toward the center. Repeat the scraping, lifting, and folding until the eggs have formed curds.

For softer eggs with small curds, stir or whisk the eggs in the pan until curds form but the eggs are still moist, 3 to 4 minutes. Some people prefer to scramble eggs over very low heat for a longer time for curds that are even more tender and fluffier.

Transfer the eggs directly to the bowls.

MANY WAYS OF TOFU

Tofu may be the easiest way to pack a protein punch into a bowl, if only because it can be sliced or diced and added raw. A little effort on the cooking front, however, will pay off big time in terms of flavor. The methods and recipes that follow assume the use of fresh block tofu packed in water. Either firm or extra firm will work best.

TIP: PRESSED TOFU

Pressing tofu gets rid of some of its liquid, making it a bit firmer and definitely less "wet." Place the tofu on a rimmed plate or soup plate or in a baking dish, set a plate, pie dish, or small cutting board on the tofu, and place a small, heavy pot, a heavy can of food, or one or more other heavy objects on top. Make sure the weight is well balanced and is not so heavy that the tofu crumbles rather just releases excess liquid. Let the setup sit at room temperature for at least 15 minutes or in the refrigerator for up to overnight. Discard any liquid that accumulates and use the tofu in the recipe at hand.

TIP: BLANCHED TOFU

Like the idea of tofu but don't care for its slightly sour taste? Select a saucepan large enough to accommodate the tofu, fill the pan with water, and bring the water to a boil. Add the tofu and simmer for about 1 minute. Using a slotted spatula, carefully lift the tofu out of the water and place on a rimmed plate or soup plate. Press the tofu as directed in Pressed Tofu (see left). Any sourness will now be noticeably, wonderfully softened.

Baked Tofu

One 8-oz [230-g] block tofu, preferably pressed (see left)

1 recipe marinade of your choice (see page 31)

Use the tofu as a whole block, cut it into eight uniform slices, or cut it into sixteen bite-size cubes. Pat the tofu dry, transfer it to a bowl, and pour the marinade over it. Cover and refrigerate for at least 30 minutes or up to overnight.

Preheat the oven to 375°F [190°C]. Generously oil a baking pan large enough to hold the tofu in a single layer.

Using a slotted utensil, lift the tofu out of the marinade, reserving the marinade, and place the tofu in a single layer in the prepared pan. Bake for 15 minutes. Flip the tofu, pour on some of the reserved marinade, and bake until the tofu is heated through, firm, and starting to brown on the edges, about 15 minutes longer. Serve

CONT'D

warm, transferring it directly to the bowls, or let cool (it will firm up even further) before adding to the bowls. If you cooked the block whole, slice or cut it as you like to add to bowls.

Grilled Tofu

One 8-oz [230-g] block tofu, pressed (see page 29)
1 recipe marinade of your choice (see page 31)

Pat the block of pressed tofu dry, put it in a bowl, and pour the marinade over it. Cover and refrigerate for at least 30 minutes or up to overnight.

Prepare a fire in a charcoal or gas grill for direct-heat cooking over medium heat. (You should be able to hold your hand about 1 in [2.5 cm] above the cooking grate for 4 to 5 seconds before you must pull it away.)

Using a slotted spoon, lift the tofu out of the marinade, reserving the marinade. Oil the cooking grate. Place the tofu on the grate directly over the fire and brush with the marinade. Grill the tofu, basting occasionally with the marinade and turning once, until grill marks are visible on both sides and the tofu is hot, 5 to 8 minutes per side. Cut into slices or cubes and add to bowls, or let it cool and firm up before cutting and serving.

The charred marks and smoky flavor of the grill add an extra oomph to mild tofu. To ensure the best result, start with a clean, well-oiled cooking grate.

Broiled Tofu

One 8-oz [230-g] block tofu, pressed (see page 29)
1 recipe marinade of your choice (see page 31)

Cut the tofu block into eight uniform slices or into sixteen bite-size cubes. Pat the tofu dry, transfer it to a bowl, and pour the marinade over it. Cover and refrigerate for at least 30 minutes or up to overnight.

Set an oven rack about 4 in [10 cm] below the heating element and preheat the broiler. Generously oil a baking sheet.

Using a slotted utensil, lift the tofu out of the marinade and arrange in a single layer in the prepared pan. Discard the marinade. Slip the pan under the broiler and broil the tofu until it starts to brown, about 4 minutes. Flip the tofu and broil until the tofu starts to brown on the second side, about 4 minutes longer. Serve warm, transferring it directly to the bowls, or let cool (it will firm up even further) before adding to the bowls.

Black Pepper Tofu (page 93)

Teriyaki Marinade

2 Tbsp soy sauce
2 Tbsp mirin
2 tsp rice vinegar
1 garlic clove, minced (optional)
2 tsp peeled and finely grated fresh ginger (optional)
1 Tbsp toasted sesame oil (if grilling the tofu)

In a small bowl, whisk together the soy sauce, mirin, vinegar, and the garlic and ginger, if using. If grilling the tofu, whisk in the sesame oil.

BBQ Marinade

¼ cup [65 g] ketchup
1 Tbsp cider vinegar
1 Tbsp brown sugar
½ tsp freshly ground black pepper
½ tsp dry mustard
1 tsp warm water (if baking the tofu)
2 Tbsp canola oil (if grilling the tofu)

In a small bowl, whisk together the ketchup, vinegar, sugar, pepper, and mustard, mixing well to dissolve the sugar. If baking the tofu, whisk in the warm water; if grilling the tofu, whisk in the canola oil.

Peanut Marinade

2 Tbsp soy sauce
2 Tbsp brown sugar
1 Tbsp toasted sesame oil
1 Tbsp peanut butter
½ tsp Sriracha sauce or garlic chile paste
1 Tbsp peanut oil (if grilling the tofu)

In a small bowl, whisk together the soy sauce, sugar, sesame oil, peanut butter, and Sriracha sauce, mixing well to dissolve the sugar. If grilling the tofu, whisk in the peanut oil.

Honey-Garlic Marinade

2 Tbsp honey
1 Tbsp soy sauce
1 garlic clove, minced
¼ tsp freshly ground black pepper
1 Tbsp canola oil (if grilling the tofu)

In a small bowl, whisk together the honey, soy sauce, garlic, and pepper. If grilling the tofu, whisk in the canola oil.

Cilantro-Lime Marinade

¼ cup [60 ml] fresh lime juice
2 Tbsp minced fresh cilantro
1 garlic clove, minced
½ tsp salt
¼ tsp cayenne pepper
1 Tbsp olive oil (if grilling the tofu)

In a small bowl, whisk together the lime juice, cilantro, garlic, salt, and cayenne. If grilling the tofu, whisk in the olive oil.

One of the great things about bowl-based meals is how they elevate otherwise humble ingredients. In the world of fish, that can mean canned tuna or sardines (I always look for olive oil–packed versions for their rich flavor) or flaked bits of smoked fish, which deliver big flavor for a small amount. Even fish left over from last night's dinner, flaked and topped with some sauce, can make a simple bowl taste fancy. A modest amount of more costly shellfish, like shrimp and scallops, can also be strategically employed to bring both flavor and a protein to otherwise humble creations. Each of the following recipes will dress four bowls modestly.

Grilled Fish

One 12-oz [340-g] fish fillet, or four 3-oz [85-g] fillets
Olive oil for brushing
Salt

Prepare a fire in a charcoal or gas grill for direct-heat cooking over medium heat. (You should be able to hold your hand about 1 in [2.5 cm] above the cooking grate for 4 to 5 seconds before you must pull it away.)

Brush the fish on both sides with olive oil and then sprinkle both sides with salt. Oil the cooking grate. If the skin is still on the fish, place the fish, skin-side down, on the grate directly over the fire. If the fish has delicate flesh, place it in a fish basket on the grate, or oil a piece of aluminum foil, poke some holes in the foil, and then place the fish on the foil on the grate. Cover and cook until the underside is grill marked, 4 to 5 minutes. If the fish is skinless, flip it, re-cover, and continue to cook until it just flakes in the center when pierced with a knife, 4 to 5 minutes longer for a piece 1 inch [2.5 cm] thick. If the skin is intact, just leave the fish cooking skin-side down in the covered grill for the least-fish-stuck-to-the-grill result. (A good general rule is to allow 10 minutes for each 1 in [2.5 cm] of thickness, though it is always best to use your eyes rather than following the clock.)

If grilling small fillet portions, transfer them directly to the bowls. If grilling a single large fillet, cut into pieces before transferring to the bowls.

Here's the great thing about grilled fish: the fishy smell stays outside. The key to grilling fish is to start with a clean, well-oiled cooking grate. That means you need to scrub the grate clean, oil it, heat the grill, and then oil the grate again.

Pan-Seared Fish

One 12-oz [340-g] fish fillet, or four 3-oz [85-g] skinless fillets
Salt
Olive oil for cooking

Season the fish on both sides with salt. Heat a large frying pan over medium heat. When the pan is hot, add enough olive oil to coat the bottom generously (about 1 Tbsp oil for a 10-in [25-cm] pan), swirling the pan to coat evenly. When the oil is hot, set the fish in the pan and let it sizzle and cook until lightly browned on the underside, 4 to 5 minutes. Using a spatula (use a large one if turning a whole fillet), turn the fish over and cook until it is browned on the second side and just flakes in the center when pierced with a knife, 4 to 5 minutes longer. (A good general rule is to allow 10 minutes for each 1 in [2.5 cm] of thickness, though it is always best to use your eyes rather than following the clock.)

If cooking small fillet portions, transfer them directly to the bowls. If cooking a single large fillet, cut into pieces before transferring to the bowls.

You can add flavor to the fish by mixing the salt with black or cayenne pepper, dried herbs, or a favorite spice rub.

Seared Tuna

12 to 16 oz [340 to 455 g] fresh tuna
¼ tsp salt
1 tsp olive oil

Sprinkle the tuna on both sides with the salt. In a medium frying pan over medium-high heat, warm the olive oil, swirling the pan to coat the bottom evenly. When the oil is hot, set the tuna in the pan; it should sizzle immediately. Let the tuna cook until a light brown crust forms on the underside, 1 to 2 minutes. Flip the tuna and cook until a light brown crust forms on the second side, 1 to 2 minutes longer. This timing will result in rare tuna, still red in the center. For medium tuna, cook for 2 to 3 minutes longer on each side.

Transfer the tuna to a cutting board and let rest for a few minutes, then cut into slices against the grain and transfer directly to the bowls.

Oil-Poached Tuna

12 to 16 oz [325 to 450 g] fresh tuna
½ tsp salt
1 cup [240 ml] olive oil
3 garlic cloves
6 black peppercorns
1 bay leaf
3 strips orange or lemon zest
1 dried hot chile (optional)

Season the tuna on both sides with the salt and set aside. In a saucepan just large enough to hold the fish in a single layer, combine the olive oil, garlic, peppercorns,

CONT'D

bay leaf, orange zest, and chile (if using). Place over medium-low heat and warm the oil just until bubbles form on the sides of the pan. Add the tuna and adjust the heat to maintain those few bubbles on the sides of the pan. Cook until the tuna is opaque at the center when pierced with the tip of knife, about 8 minutes for a piece 1 in [2.5 cm] thick.

Have ready a cooling rack set on a rimmed baking sheet. When the tuna is ready, using a large spatula or shallow slotted spoon, lift the tuna out of the oil and onto the cooling rack to drain briefly. Transfer the tuna to a cutting board, cut into slices against the grain, and transfer directly to the bowls. Or, use two forks to flake the tuna into large chunks and then transfer to the bowls.

Grilled Shrimp

2 lb [910 g] shell-on shrimp
2 Tbsp butter, melted, or olive oil

Prepare a fire in a charcoal or gas grill for direct-heat cooking over medium-high heat. (You should be able to hold your hand about 1 in [2.5 cm] above the cooking grate for 3 to 4 seconds before you must pull it away.)

Thread the shrimp onto metal skewers or place in a grilling basket. Oil the cooking grate. Brush the shrimp on all sides with some of the butter and set on the cooking grate directly over the fire. Cook until the shrimp start to turn pink, about 1 minute. Brush with more of the butter, then flip

the shrimp and cook until just cooked through; this usually takes 1 to 2 minutes, depending on the size of the shrimp. Be careful not to overcook, as the shrimp can get very tough. Transfer to a plate and brush with any remaining butter before adding to bowls.

VARIATIONS

To make lemon shrimp, combine the butter with the finely grated zest of 1 lemon and 2 tsp fresh lemon juice.

To make ginger shrimp, combine the butter with 2 tsp peeled and finely grated fresh ginger.

Roasted Shrimp

2 lb [910 g] peeled and deveined shrimp
½ tsp salt
¼ tsp freshly ground black pepper

Preheat the oven to 400°F [200°C].

Toss the shrimp with the salt and pepper and spread in a single layer on a baking sheet. Roast until cooked through, 5 to 10 minutes, depending on the size of the shrimp. Transfer directly to the bowls.

Pickled Shrimp

4 cups [960 ml] water
1 Tbsp plus 1 tsp salt
1 lb [455 g] large (21/25 count) peeled and deveined shrimp
¼ cup [60 ml] white wine vinegar
½ cup [120 ml] fresh lemon juice
1 tsp sugar

Combine the water and the 1 Tbsp salt in a medium saucepan and bring to a boil over high heat. While the water is heating, fill a large bowl with ice water and set it near the stove. When the water is at a rolling boil, remove the pan from the heat and add the shrimp. Leave the shrimp in the water until they turn pink and opaque, about 5 minutes. Using a slotted spoon, transfer the just-cooked shrimp to the ice water. Reserve ½ cup [120 ml] of the shrimp cooking water.

Arrange a double or triple layer of paper towels on a large platter. When the shrimp are cool, transfer them to the paper towels and turn them as needed to pat dry. In a medium bowl, combine the vinegar, lemon juice, sugar, and the remaining 1 tsp salt, whisking to dissolve the sugar and salt. Whisk in the reserved shrimp cooking water. Set the bowl in the ice-water bath and leave until cold. Add the shrimp and stir to coat with the marinade. Cover and refrigerate the shrimp for at least 1 hour or up to 2 days. Just before serving, toss thoroughly to coat evenly, then transfer to the bowls.

VARIATION
To spice up the shrimp, add 1 fresh hot chile, finely chopped, to the marinade.

Poached Shrimp

2 lb [910 g] peeled and deveined shrimp
2 tsp salt

In a wide medium saucepan or pot, combine the shrimp with water to cover. Using a slotted spoon, lift the shrimp out of the pan and set aside. Bring the water in the pan to a simmer over medium heat. Add the salt and stir to dissolve. Add the shrimp, cover, and remove from the heat.

Let sit for 5 minutes, then drain. Transfer the warm shrimp directly to the bowls, or hold the shrimp under cool running water until cold, then store in an airtight container in the refrigerator for up to 2 days and use chilled.

Seared Scallops

1 lb [455 g] sea scallops
1 Tbsp butter
1 Tbsp olive oil
Salt

Check the scallops, and if they look at all gritty, rinse them. Pat the scallops thoroughly dry with paper towels. (Drying them will help them to sear better.) In a large frying pan over medium-high heat, melt the butter. When the butter stops foaming, add the olive oil. When the oil shimmers, add the scallops in a single layer, spacing them evenly apart. As they cook, sprinkle them lightly with salt. Cook until browned on the underside, 2 to 4 minutes. Using a spatula, flip the scallops and cook until browned on the second side and just barely cooked through, 2 to 4 minutes longer. Transfer directly to the bowls.

Ceviche (page 101)

Maple-Glazed Salmon (page 104)

Marinated Mussels (page 99)

Smoked Paprika Shrimp (page 96)

Bowls can be an excellent way to focus on plant-based foods, but if you are a carnivore, there's plenty of room for meat or poultry in the bowl, too. Shredded meat from a rotisserie chicken or a home-roasted bird and chopped turkey breast bought at the deli counter are two of the easiest ways to pack some protein into a bowl. But quickly cooking ground meat is easy, too, as are kebabs and meatballs and shredded or chopped cooked meat. Bowls may be, hands down, absolutely the best use of small amounts of leftovers! Bite-size is, as is almost always the case in the world of bowl cuisine, the key. Each recipe here delivers a nice amount of bird or meat protein for four bowls, with the exception of the whole roast chicken, which will vary depending on the size of the bird.

Roast Chicken

One 4-lb [1.8-kg] whole chicken
2 tsp salt
2 Tbsp olive oil or butter
1 cup [240 ml] dry white wine or chicken broth

Pat the chicken dry with paper towels. Using your fingers, carefully loosen the skin from the meat on the breasts and thighs. Rub the salt all over the chicken, including under the loosened skin. Set the chicken breast-side up in a roasting pan and refrigerate, uncovered, for up to 36 hours. (Leaving it uncovered will lead to a crispier skin once it's roasted, but you can cover it if you like.)

Preheat the oven to 400°F [200°C]. While the oven heats, set the chicken out at room temperature to take off the chill.

Rub the chicken breasts and the tops of the thighs with the olive oil. Pour the wine into the bottom of the pan. Roast the chicken, undisturbed, until browned, about 45 minutes.

Lower the oven temperature to 325°F [165°C], spoon some pan juices over the chicken, and continue roasting until the meat pulls away from the ends of the drumsticks and the thigh joints feel loose and move easily when you wiggle the end of a drumstick, about 30 minutes longer. (Cooking times for chicken vary greatly depending on size, temperature going into the oven, and precision of oven temperature, so go by how the chicken looks and feels, not the clock.)

Remove from the oven and let the chicken rest in the pan for about 10 minutes. Transfer the chicken to a large cutting board and cut into smallish pieces to add to the bowls. Or, for shredded chicken, let the bird cool completely, remove the skin and pull the meat off the bones with your fingers or a fork. If you have more chicken than you need for a single meal, pack the leftover pieces or meat in an airtight container and refrigerate for up to 3 days.

NOTE: You can adjust this recipe for different-size chickens. Use ½ tsp salt for each 1 lb [455 g] chicken. The butter or oil and the wine or broth amounts can remain the same. Plan on 18 to 20 minutes per pound.

VARIATIONS

Lemon Chicken Halve 1 lemon, squeeze the juice from the halves all over the bird, and then stuff the spent halves into the cavity.

Garlic Chicken Mince 1 to 2 garlic cloves and rub all over the chicken and/or stuff the cavity with 1 head garlic, separated into cloves and peeled.

Herb Chicken Carefully tuck a handful of fresh herbs (thyme or parsley is a good choice) under the skin. Add more to the cavity, if you like.

Cayenne Chicken Mix ¼ to ½ tsp cayenne pepper with the salt to add a bit of spicy heat.

Paprika Chicken Mix about 1 tsp paprika with the salt. Use smoked paprika, if possible, for a delightful light smoky flavor.

Roast Chicken Thighs and/or Breasts

2 bone-in, skin-on chicken thighs and/or breasts
1 tsp salt
Olive oil or melted butter for brushing

Preheat the oven to 425°F [220°C]. Oil a baking pan just large enough to accommodate the chicken pieces in a single layer without touching.

Pat the chicken pieces dry with paper towels and put them in the prepared baking pan. Sprinkle the chicken evenly on all sides with the salt and let sit for 30 minutes. Brush or rub the pieces with the olive oil and then arrange them, skin-side up, in the pan.

Roast until well browned and cooked through when tested with a knife, 20 to 30 minutes. Remove the chicken from the oven and let cool until it can be handled, then remove the skin, pull the meat off the bones, and add the meat directly to the bowls.

Chicken thighs will likely need more time than breasts to cook through, but you can still cook them together and just remove the breasts from the oven when they're done.

Mirin-Braised Chicken Thighs (page 123)
Paprika-Braised Chicken (page 121)
Yogurt-Marinated Chicken (page 110)

Basic Ground Meat

1 tsp olive or cooking oil
1 small onion, minced
½ tsp salt
1 lb [455 g] ground beef, chicken, lamb, pork, or turkey

In a large frying pan over medium-high heat, warm the oil. Add the onion and salt and cook, stirring, until the onion is soft, about 3 minutes. Add the meat and cook, stirring now and again and breaking up the meat as it cooks, until the meat is browned and cooked through, about 5 minutes. If the cooked meat seems too fatty, spoon out and discard the excess fat or drain the meat on a doubled or tripled layer of paper towels before adding it to the bowls.

VARIATIONS

Add 1 to 2 garlic cloves, finely chopped, with the onion.

Throw in a small handful of chopped fresh herbs (such as parsley, mint, or cilantro) just as the meat is done cooking.

Taco it up by adding 1 tsp ground cumin and ¼ tsp cayenne pepper just before you add the meat to the pan.

Sprinkle 1 Tbsp fresh lime juice over the meat just before removing from the heat.

Use 2 to 3 green onions, white and green parts, minced, in place of the onion.

Add 1 tsp peeled and finely grated fresh ginger with the onion and use 1 tsp soy sauce in place of the salt.

Spiced Ground Turkey (page 117)

Meatballs

1 lb [455 g] ground beef, chicken, lamb, pork, or turkey
½ tsp salt
½ small onion or 1 shallot, minced
¼ cup [10 g] chopped fresh herbs (such as parsley, thyme, or dill)
Olive or other cooking oil for cooking

Put the meat in a large bowl and sprinkle with the salt, onion, and herbs. Use your hands to pull the meat into small bits and mix with the seasonings. Divide into eight, twelve, or sixteen equal portions, roll each portion into a ball, and set the balls on a large plate or baking sheet. Cover and chill for at least 30 minutes (chilled meatballs hold their shape better as they cook).

Have ready a large platter lined with a double or triple layer of paper towels. Place a large frying pan or wide, shallow saucepan over medium-high heat. Add enough oil to coat the bottom of the pan evenly. When the oil is hot, add the meatballs and cook, turning them as they brown on each side, until browned all over and cooked through, 8 to 12 minutes total, depending on their size. Using a slotted spoon, transfer the meatballs to the towel-lined platter to drain briefly before plopping them into bowls.

Minted Meatballs (page 143)

Meat or Chicken on Skewers

1 lb [455 g] boneless beef, lamb, pork, or chicken, cut into large bite-size pieces
½ tsp salt
Olive oil for tossing

Put the meat in a bowl and sprinkle with the salt. Toss to distribute the salt evenly. Cover and refrigerate for at least 10 minutes or up to overnight. Drizzle with a glug or two of olive oil, toss to coat the meat evenly, and thread onto four skewers. (If using bamboo, rather than metal, skewers, be sure to soak them in water for about 30 minutes before sliding on the meat.)

NOTE: The following instructions assume you want the meat cooked through. If you are cooking beef or lamb and would prefer it cooked less, shorten the cooking time by 1 to 2 minutes on each side.

TO GRILL: Prepare a fire in a charcoal or gas grill for direct-heat cooking over high heat. (You should be able to hold your hand about 1 in [2.5 cm] above the cooking grate for 1 to 2 seconds before you must pull it away.) Oil the cooking grate. Set the oiled skewers on the grate directly over the fire and cook until browned on the underside, 4 to 5 minutes. Flip the skewers and grill until browned on the second side and cooked through, 4 to 5 minutes longer.

TO PANFRY: Place a large frying pan (large enough to hold the skewers) over high heat. Lightly coat the bottom of the pan with olive oil. When the oil is hot, add the skewers to the pan, lower the heat to medium-high, and cook until the meat is browned on the underside, 4 to 5 minutes. Flip the skewers and cook until browned on the second side and cooked through, 4 to 5 minutes longer.

TO BROIL: Set an oven rack about 4 in [10 cm] from the heating element and preheat the broiler. Set the skewers on a broiler pan or baking sheet. Slip the pan under the broiler and broil, watching carefully to avoid burning, until browned, 4 to 5 minutes. Flip the skewers and broil until browned on the second side and cooked through, 4 to 5 minutes longer.

However you cook the skewers, let them rest for about 10 minutes before serving, then either place a skewer in each bowl or slide the pieces off the skewers into the bowls.

VARIATIONS

Add mushrooms, chunks of zucchini, cherry tomatoes, or other quick-cooking vegetables to the skewers.

Throw in a small handful of one or more chopped fresh herbs (such as rosemary or thyme) along with the salt.

Sprinkle the meat with about ½ tsp ground spice or a mixture (such as cumin, coriander, paprika and/or cayenne pepper) with the salt.

Marinate the meat before skewering. Any of the tofu marinades on page 31 can be used here.

Shredded Meat
(aka The Best Ever Use of Leftovers!)

2 to 4 oz [55 to 115 g] cooked meat of any kind per person

Use two forks (or your fingers) to pull the meat into shreds. Add to the bowls.

If you have more leftover meat than you can use in a night or two, you can shred it and freeze it in an airtight container for up to 2 months. Freezing will dry the meat out a bit, however, so be sure to reheat it with a little broth to liven it up.

Soupy Braised Pork (page 127)

Steak

12 to 16 oz [340 to 455 g] steak (filet mignon, sirloin, or New York strip), about 1 in [2.5 cm] thick
¼ tsp salt
Freshly ground black pepper (optional)
Olive or other cooking oil for brushing

Sprinkle the steak on both sides with the salt and let it sit at room temperature for 15 to 30 minutes. You want the salt to season the meat, and you want the meat to come close to room temperature before you cook it. Season with pepper, if you like, and then brush all over with a little oil.

TO GRILL: Prepare a fire in a charcoal or gas grill for direct-heat cooking over high heat. (You should be able to hold your hand about 1 in [2.5 cm] above the cooking grate for 1 to 2 seconds before you must pull it away.) Oil the cooking grate. Set the steak on the grate directly over the fire and cook until grill marks form on the underside, 4 to 5 minutes for rare, 6 to 7 minutes for medium, and 8 to 9 minutes for well-done. Flip the steak and cook until grill marks form on the second side and the steak is done to your liking, 4 to 5 minutes longer for rare, 6 to 7 minutes longer for medium, and 8 to 9 minutes longer for well-done.

TO PANFRY: Heat a large frying pan over high heat. Lightly coat the bottom of the pan with oil. When the oil is hot, add the steak, lower the heat to medium-high, and cook until browned on the underside, 4 to 5 minutes for rare, 6 to 7 minutes for medium, and 8 to 9 minutes for well-done. Flip the steak and cook until browned on the second side and done to your liking, 4 to 5 minutes longer for rare, 6 to 7 minutes longer for medium, and 8 to 9 minutes longer for well-done.

TO BROIL: Set an oven rack about 4 in [10 cm] from the heating element and preheat the broiler. Set the steak on a broiler pan or baking sheet. Slip the pan under the broiler and broil, watching carefully to avoid burning, until browned, 4 to 5 minutes for rare, 6 to 7 minutes for medium, and 8 to 9 minutes for well-done. Flip the steak and broil on the second side until browned and done to your liking, 4 to 5 minutes longer for rare, 6 to 7 minutes longer for medium, and 8 to 9 minutes longer for well-done.

However you cook the steak, let it rest for 10 to 15 minutes before you slice it against the grain and add it to the bowls.

Eating by the bowl lets you serve less meat per person, making items like a good steak more affordable. As with the other meats in this book, I usually plan on 3 to 4 oz [85 to 115 g] per serving, which means a single 1-lb [455-g] steak will easily feed four.

Korean-Spiced Steak (page 139)

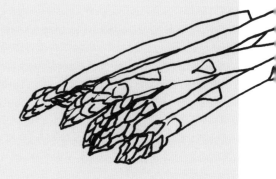

FOR THE LOVE OF VEGETABLES

Getting lots of vegetables into your diet is a great reason to turn to bowls. The rule here is that there is no rule. Raw vegetables that are chopped, sliced, or shredded into bite-size pieces are the way to go, but so are freshly prepared or leftover cooked vegetables of all sorts. Mixing raw, roasted, grilled, and steamed vegetables adds color, nutrition, taste, and texture, so use your imagination— and what's in your refrigerator—to come up with healthful and delicious combinations.

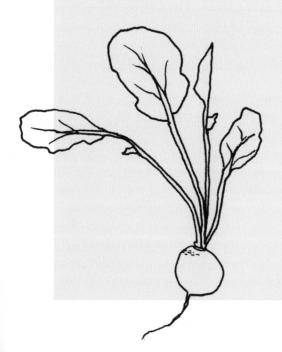

If you're using raw vegetables, the big question will be whether to slice or chop. Slicing tends to yield vegetables that are crisp, while chopped vegetables are typically crunchy, so it's all about which texture you want to add.

Consider these raw vegetables for your bowls: bell peppers, broccoli, cabbage, carrots, cauliflower, corn kernels (yes, raw!), cucumber, fennel, kale, lettuces of all sorts, radishes, spinach, sweet peas, tomatoes, turnips (baby turnips are wonderful raw), zucchini and other summer squashes.

I tend to leave the peel, or skin, on if it is at all edible, preferring to scrub vegetables clean rather than peel them when I'm eating them raw. But whether to peel or not is, of course, up to you. (I do always peel raw broccoli stems, as the tough peel conceals a wonderful tender and sweet core.)

Roasted Vegetables

4 cups [455 to 560 g] chopped vegetables (see note)
Olive oil for drizzling
Salt

Preheat the oven to between 350°F [180°C] and 425°F [220°C]. I offer a range because vegetables will roast up browner and faster at a higher temperature, but they will roast up tender and lovely anywhere between those two points.

Put the vegetables in a roasting pan or a large baking sheet, drizzle with olive oil, and toss to coat evenly. Spread the pieces in a single layer, sprinkle with salt, and roast until tender and browned. This will take anywhere from 15 minutes for asparagus or cherry tomatoes up to 30 minutes for beets and other root vegetables and many winter squashes, depending on how browned you want them, how hot the oven is, and how tender you want them. Transfer directly to the bowls. Serve warm or at room temperature.

Consider these vegetables for roasting: asparagus, beets, broccoli, Brussels sprouts, cabbage (in wedges), carrots, cauliflower, chiles, fennel, green beans, kale, mushrooms, okra, onions, parsnips, potatoes, rutabagas, sweet potatoes, tomatoes, turnips, winter squashes (including sweet pumpkins), zucchini and other summer squashes.

bowl basics

43

Grilled Vegetables

Vegetable or vegetables of choice, whole (if small) or cut in half, into quarters, or even into slices for larger vegetables (see note)
Olive oil for brushing
Salt

Prepare a fire in a charcoal or gas grill for direct-heat cooking over medium-high heat. (You should be able to hold your hand about 1 in [2.5 cm] above the cooking grate for 3 to 4 seconds before you must pull it away.) Oil the cooking grate.

Spread the vegetables on a baking sheet or large platter. Brush or drizzle evenly with olive oil and sprinkle with salt. Set the vegetables on the cooking grate directly over the fire and cook, undisturbed, until grill marks form on the underside, 4 to 8 minutes, depending on the vegetable. Flip and cook until they have grill marks on the second side and are tender, 4 to 8 minutes longer, depending on the vegetable. Return the vegetables to the baking sheet or platter and cut into bite-size slices or chunks before adding to the bowls. Serve warm or at room temperature.

Consider these vegetables for grilling: asparagus, beets, Brussels sprouts (seriously!), eggplant, green beans, mushrooms, okra, potatoes, spring onions, tomatoes, zucchini, winter squashes (including sweet pumpkins).

Steamed Vegetables

4 cups [455 to 560 g] vegetables, in slices, chunks, or florets (see note)

WITH A STEAM BASKET OR COLANDER: Select a pot into which the basket or colander will fit. Pour water into the pot to a depth of 1 in [2.5 cm] (the water must not touch the bottom of the basket or colander once it is added). Bring the water to a boil over high heat. Put the vegetables in the basket or colander (if steaming more than one type of vegetable, keep like with like so you can take out the ones that are done first), set it over the boiling water, cover, and cook.

WITHOUT A STEAM BASKET OR COLANDER: Pour water to a depth of ¼ in [6 mm] into a large frying pan and bring the water to a boil over high heat. Add the vegetables, cover, turn the heat to low, and cook.

With either cooking method, cook the vegetables until they are crisp-tender or tender to the bite, as you prefer. Start checking after 3 minutes. The timing varies greatly depending on the type of vegetable, so follow your palate and not the clock. Transfer the vegetables directly to the bowls. Serve warm or at room temperature.

Consider these vegetables for steaming: asparagus, beets, broccoli, carrots, cauliflower, edamame, fiddlehead ferns, green beans, small or new potatoes, snap peas.

Root Vegetable Hash

About 2 lb [910 g] root vegetables
2 Tbsp canola or vegetable oil
½ tsp salt

Peel the vegetables and grate them on the large holes of a box grater. Rinse in cool water, drain, and squeeze dry with your hands or roll up in a kitchen towel or layers of paper towels and squeeze out any excess moisture.

Heat the oil in a large frying pan over medium-high heat. Add the vegetables, spreading them evenly over the bottom of the pan, cover, lower the heat to medium, and cook until browned on the underside, about 5 minutes. Uncover and sprinkle evenly with the salt. Using a spatula, turn the vegetables over and continue to cook, uncovered, until browned on the second side and tender, about 5 minutes longer. Transfer directly to the bowls.

This simple hash is traditionally made with potatoes, but other root vegetables work just as well (sweet potatoes!), particularly in combination with each other, such as parsnips and beets, or celery root and turnips. Both single-vegetable hashes and mixed-vegetable hashes make especially tasty nongrain bases for simple bowls.

Mashed Cauliflower

2 Tbsp butter
1 garlic clove, minced
1 head cauliflower, florets and stems chopped
½ tsp fine sea salt
⅓ cup [80 ml] water
3 Tbsp heavy cream (optional)

In a large frying pan over medium-high heat, melt the butter. Add the garlic and cook, stirring as it sizzles, until fragrant, about 30 seconds. Add the cauliflower and stir to coat with the butter. Sprinkle with the salt and add the water. Cover, turn the heat to medium-low, and cook until the cauliflower is so tender you can mash it easily with a fork, 20 to 30 minutes.

Uncover, add the cream, if using, and stir to coat the cauliflower evenly with the cream. The cauliflower should now be so tender that even stirring it lightly causes it to break up a bit. Cook off any excess liquid in the pan, then remove from the heat.

Using a large fork or a potato masher, mash the cauliflower. I tend to like mine pretty chunky; for a smoother mash, you can whirl it in a food processor. Transfer the cauliflower directly to the bowls.

Mashed Potatoes

2 lb [910 g] russet or Yukon Gold potatoes
Salt
½ cup [120 ml] whole milk, half-and-half,
or heavy cream (or make it tangy with
buttermilk, plain yogurt, or sour cream)
2 to 3 Tbsp butter

Put the potatoes in a large pot, add water
to cover, and place over high heat. Bring
to a boil, add 1 Tbsp salt, adjust the heat
to maintain a steady low boil, and cook
until the potatoes are tender all the way
through when pierced with a knife. Start
checking after about 20 minutes; large
potatoes could take up to 45 minutes. The
knife should meet with no resistance. This
is a case where a bit overcooked is better
than a bit undercooked.

Meanwhile, in a small saucepan over low
heat, warm the milk until steaming hot (or
put in a microwave-safe bowl and heat
in a microwave). Pour the hot milk into a
large bowl. Cut up the butter into small
pieces and add the pieces to the milk.

Drain the potatoes, return them to the hot
pot, place over low heat, and heat, shaking
the pot frequently, to dry the potatoes
a bit. Less moisture in the potatoes will
result in fluffier mashed potatoes.

If you are lucky enough to own a ricer,
position it over the bowl holding the milk
and butter and pass the potatoes, one at
a time, through the ricer into the bowl.
(If the potatoes are large, you may need
to cut them into pieces to fit them in the
ricer.) Once all of the potatoes are in the
bowl, stir or whisk together the potatoes,
milk, and butter until smooth. If you don't
have a ricer, put on an oven mitt, grab a
potato with the gloved hand, and with a
paring knife in your other hand, scrape off
the skin. Drop the peeled potato into the
bowl and repeat with the remaining potatoes. Use a potato masher or a large fork
to mash the potatoes with the milk and
butter until as smooth as possible. Season
with salt and transfer directly to the bowls.

Other potato-like root vegetables, such
as sweet potatoes and turnips, can also be
mashed. They tend to cook up better if they
are cut into even chunks before boiling, but
otherwise proceed as for potatoes, peeling
them if needed. You can also mix potatoes
with another root vegetable, replacing up to
half the amount of potatoes with celery root,
for example, or even beets, if you dare serve
something so pink!

Sautéed Greens

1 bunch cooking greens, such as kale, collards, Swiss chard, or broccoli rabe
1 Tbsp olive, coconut, or other cooking oil
¼ tsp salt
¼ cup [60 ml] water

Cut off and discard the tough stem ends from the greens, then cut the remaining stems from the leaves. Chop the stems and leaves, keeping them separate. (Some people choose to discard the stems, and you can too, but they are perfectly edible, so I like to use them.) Place a large frying pan or sauté pan over medium-high heat and add the oil. When the oil shimmers, add the chopped stems and salt and cook, stirring, until they brighten in color, about 1 minute. Add the water, cover, turn the heat to low, and cook until the stems are just tender to the bite, 5 to 10 minutes; the timing will depend on the type of greens.

Uncover, add the chopped greens, stir to combine, raise the heat to medium, and cook, stirring frequently, until the greens are wilted and tender, about 3 minutes for chard and up to 10 minutes or longer for kale or collards. Transfer directly to the bowls, or have them ready while you get other ingredients together and serve at room temperature.

VARIATIONS

Add 1 garlic clove, sliced, with the stems.
Add about ½ teaspoon peeled and finely grated fresh ginger with the greens.
Sprinkle in ¼ tsp red pepper flakes with the stems.
Grate lemon zest to taste over the finished greens.
Drizzle extra-virgin olive oil over the finished greens.

Spaghetti Squash

One 3- to 4-lb [1.4- to 1.8-kg] spaghetti squash

Preheat the oven to 375°F [190°C] and oil a baking sheet. Cut off and discard the ends of the squash and then cut the squash in half lengthwise. Scoop out and discard the seeds and set both halves, cut-side down, on the prepared baking sheet. Roast until the squash is tender when pierced with a fork, 45 to 60 minutes.

Remove from the oven and turn the halves cut-side up. Using a fork, scoop out flesh in spaghetti-like strands and use them as a base or to top your bowls.

Winter Squash Mash

One 3- to 4-lb [1.3 to 1.8-kg] winter squash
2 Tbsp butter
¼ to ½ cup [60 to 120 ml] whole milk or
heavy cream, warmed (optional)
Salt

Trim off the ends of the squash, then peel
off the skin using a paring knife or a vegetable peeler. Cut the squash in half lengthwise and scoop out and discard the seeds
and fibrous pulp. Cut into even cubes.
Boil, steam, or microwave the squash
pieces until tender when pierced with a
knife tip.

Transfer the squash cubes to a large bowl,
add the butter, and, using a large fork or
a potato masher, mash until the squash is
smooth and the butter has melted. Pour
in the milk for extra richness, if desired,
and stir to combine. Spoon into the bowls
as a delicious comfort-food base. Store
any leftover mash in an airtight container
in the refrigerator for up to 3 days in the
freezer for up to 6 months.

MORE VEGETABLE RECIPES

In Part 3, you'll find plenty of additional
vegetable bases and vegetable toppings to
incorporate into your own bowl creations.

VEGETABLE BASES

More vegetables as bases:
Cabbage Kale Slaw (page 112)
Spiced Cauliflower "Couscous" (page 146)
Ribboned Kale (page 139)
Spicy Sautéed Corn (page 110)
Zucchini Noodles (page 117)

VEGETABLE TOPPINGS

More vegetables to top your bowls:
Baked Eggplant (page 143)
Burst Tomatoes (page 81)
Carrot Daikon Slaw (page 93)
Charred Vegetables (page 133)
Chopped Cilantro Salad (page 101)
Chopped Cucumber Salad (page 143)
Cucumber Tomato Salad (page 78)
Escarole Salad (page 96)
Ezme Salad (page 110)
Fennel–Green Apple Salad (page 104)
Garlic-Braised Artichokes (page 146)
Garlicky Chard (page 129)
Kimchi-Style Brussels Sprouts (page 139)
Lemony Carrots (page 115)
Marinated Mushrooms (page 115)
Moroccan-Spiced Root Vegetables (page 87)
Pickled Turnips with Their Greens (page 127)
Roasted Eggplant Salad (page 149)
Roasted Red Onions (page 139)
Shredded Romaine Salad (page 84)
Seared Brussels Sprout Leaf Salad (page 123)
Shaved Zucchini Salad (page 81)
Steamed Beets with Their Greens (page 107)
Sweet Pepper Slaw (page 121)
Tomato Confit (page 99)
Turmeric Vegetables (page 84)
Tzatziki (page 110)
Wilted Frisée (page 91)

SUPER SAUCES

Not that you haven't layered in lots of flavors
already, but these sauces will kick up your
bowls to the next level. Remember, adding a
sauce of some sort is the easiest way to bring
a bowl together. Many store-bought sauces—
Sriracha, hot chile oil, toasted sesame oil,
ponzu, sweet-and-sour sauce, various salad
dressings—are quick and delicious ways to
go. Here, I've gathered some of my favorite
homemade flavor bombs for when you have
a little time to put together your own sauces.
Unless otherwise noted, these sauces are
best when freshly made, but can be covered
and refrigerated for a day or two. Each sauce
recipe makes enough for four generous servings, often with a bit left over for an ad hoc
bowl made the next day.

Aioli

1 egg

1 Tbsp fresh lemon juice, plus more if needed for thinning

1 garlic clove, crushed or minced

½ tsp Dijon mustard

½ to ¾ cup [120 to 180 ml] olive oil or mixture of olive oil and canola or other neutral vegetable oil

Salt

In a blender or food processor, whirl together the egg, lemon juice, garlic, and mustard until blended. With the motor running on low speed, slowly add the oil, a drop or two at a time, allowing each addition to incorporate into the egg mixture before adding more. Once the mixture has emulsified, thickened, and lightened in color, you can begin adding the remaining oil in a slow, steady stream. Use only as much of the oil as needed to achieve a good mayonnaise consistency. When the oil has been incorporated, season the mixture with salt. If the sauce it is too thick, thin with a few drops of lemon juice (although counterintuitive, more oil will thicken the mixture).

Avocado Vinaigrette

½ ripe avocado, peeled

1 small shallot, minced

1 Tbsp red wine vinegar or fresh lime juice

1 tsp Dijon mustard

¼ tsp salt

3 Tbsp extra-virgin olive oil

In a bowl, mash the avocado with a fork until fairly smooth. Add the shallot, vinegar, mustard, and salt. Mash and stir until a smooth paste forms. Stir in the olive oil to make a smooth dressing.

Basil Pesto

Leaves from 2 bunches basil

2 to 4 garlic cloves, chopped

½ cup [120 ml] extra-virgin olive oil

2 Tbsp fresh lemon juice

Salt

¼ cup [30 g] pine nuts

½ cup [40 g] shredded Parmesan cheese

¼ to ½ cup [60 to 120 ml] lukewarm water

To keep the basil as bright green as possible, follow this optional blanching step: Bring a large pot of salted water to a boil and prepare a bowl of ice water. Dunk the basil leaves in the boiling water for 30 seconds, drain, and immediately plunge them into the ice water to cool them off. Drain and squeeze dry.

In a blender or food processor, whirl together the basil, garlic, olive oil, lemon juice, and salt until smooth. Add the nuts and Parmesan and pulse until the nuts are incorporated. Transfer to a bowl and stir in as much of the water as needed to create a level of sauciness you like.

Basil Vinaigrette

Leaves from 1 large bunch basil
1 garlic clove, minced
2 Tbsp white wine or champagne vinegar
¼ cup [60 ml] extra-virgin olive oil
Salt and freshly ground black pepper

In a blender or food processor, whirl together the basil, garlic, and vinegar until thoroughly blended. With the motor running, drizzle in the oil. Season with salt and pepper.

Caper Dressing

2 Tbsp drained capers, minced
1 small shallot, minced
3 Tbsp extra-virgin olive oil
1 Tbsp white wine vinegar or champagne vinegar
½ tsp dry mustard
Salt and freshly ground black pepper

In a small bowl, whisk together the capers, shallot, olive oil, vinegar, and mustard until well blended. Season with salt and pepper.

Chimichurri

2 garlic cloves
1 cup [30 g] packed fresh flat-leaf parsley leaves
½ cup [10 g] packed fresh cilantro leaves
½ cup [120 ml] extra-virgin olive oil
⅓ cup [80 ml] red wine vinegar
½ tsp ground cumin
½ tsp salt
½ tsp red pepper flakes

Put the garlic in a food processor and pulse until the garlic is finely chopped, stopping to scrape down the sides as needed. Add the parsley and cilantro and pulse until the herbs and garlic are minced, again stopping to scrape down the sides as needed. Add the olive oil, vinegar, cumin, and salt and pulse to combine. Pulse in the red pepper flakes.

Creamy Dill Sauce

½ cup [120 ml] buttermilk
⅓ cup [80 g] mayonnaise
2 Tbsp chopped fresh dill
2 Tbsp chopped fresh chives
1 tsp salt
¼ to ½ tsp garlic powder (optional)

In a medium bowl, whisk together the buttermilk and mayonnaise. Stir in the dill, chives, and salt. Add the garlic powder to taste (if using). Cover and refrigerate for at least 30 minutes or up to 1 week before using.

Feta Vinaigrette

¾ cup [125 g] crumbled feta cheese
⅓ cup [80 ml] extra-virgin olive oil
3 Tbsp red wine vinegar
Salt and freshly ground black pepper

In a blender food or food processor, whirl together the cheese, olive oil, and vinegar until smooth. Alternatively, in a bowl with a fork, mash together the cheese, olive oil, and vinegar until smooth. Season with salt and pepper.

Ginger Vinaigrette

1- to 2-in [2.5- to 5-cm] piece fresh ginger, peeled
¼ cup [60 ml] rice vinegar
1 Tbsp sugar
¼ cup [60 ml] cold-pressed sesame oil (not toasted!)
½ tsp soy sauce

Using the fine holes on a box grater or a rasp-type Microplane grater, finely grate the ginger into a small bowl. Add the vinegar, sugar, sesame oil, and soy sauce and stir until the sugar dissolves. Taste and adjust with more sugar and/or soy sauce if you like.

Green Garlic Sauce

1 Tbsp vegetable oil
8 oz [230 g] green garlic, white and green parts, finely chopped
½ tsp salt
¼ cup [30 g] pine nuts or pistachios
¼ cup [60 ml] extra-virgin olive oil
¼ cup [20 g] shredded aged pecorino cheese

In a large frying pan over medium-high heat, combine the vegetable oil, green garlic, and salt and cook, stirring frequently, until the green garlic is soft, about 3 minutes. Remove from the heat and let cool to warm room temperature.

In a blender or food processor, pulse the pine nuts until chopped. Transfer to a small bowl. Add the cooked green garlic to the blender or processor and whirl until bright green and smooth, stopping to scrape down the sides as necessary. With the motor running, drizzle in the olive oil and process until fully incorporated. Add the reserved nuts and the cheese and pulse until well blended. Taste and adjust with more salt, if you like.

Green Olive Sauce

18 green olives, pitted
1 garlic clove
¼ tsp salt
2 Tbsp extra-virgin olive oil
2 Tbsp sherry vinegar or fresh lemon juice
Freshly ground black pepper

On a cutting board and using a sharp knife, mince together the olives, garlic, and salt into a paste. (Or, if you have a mortar and pestle, this is a good time to use it!) Transfer the paste to a medium bowl and whisk in the olive oil and vinegar. Season with pepper.

Harissa

2 oz [55 g] large dried red chiles (New Mexican chiles work nicely here)
Boiling water to cover
4 garlic cloves, chopped
Leaves from 4 fresh flat-leaf parsley sprigs
16 large fresh mint leaves
2 Tbsp extra-virgin olive oil, plus more if needed for storing
1 Tbsp fresh lemon juice
Fine sea salt

Stem and seed the chiles. Put the chiles in a medium heatproof bowl and pour in boiling water to cover. Let the chiles soak until soft and pliable, about 30 minutes. Drain, reserving 1 cup [240 ml] of the soaking liquid.

In a blender or food processor, whirl together the soaked chiles, garlic, parsley, mint, olive oil, lemon juice, and ½ tsp salt until a smooth paste forms. Add

2 to 3 Tbsp of the soaking liquid to thin the mixture if needed to help it blend smoothly. Taste and add more olive oil, lemon juice, and salt if needed.

Transfer the sauce to a jar with a tight-fitting lid or other sealable container and store in the refrigerator for up to 2 weeks. To store the sauce for up to 1 month, top it with thin layer of olive oil before capping tightly.

Herb Butter Sauce

3 Tbsp butter
1 shallot, minced
¼ cup [60 ml] dry white vermouth or dry white wine
2 Tbsp finely chopped fresh flat-leaf parsley
2 Tbsp finely chopped fresh chives
¼ tsp finely grated lemon zest
Salt and freshly ground black pepper

In a small frying pan over medium heat, melt 1½ Tbsp of the butter. Add the shallot and cook, stirring frequently, until it softens, about 2 minutes. Add the vermouth and simmer until the liquid is reduced by about half, about 2 minutes. Meanwhile, cut the remaining 1½ Tbsp butter into small pieces. Add the parsley, chives, and lemon zest to the pan and stir just to combine. Turn the heat to low, add the butter pieces, and whisk constantly until the butter melts into the sauce. Remove from the heat and use immediately (this sauce is especially good spooned over fish, shellfish, and steamed vegetables).

Lemon Garlic Vinaigrette

2 to 3 Tbsp extra-virgin olive oil
1 Tbsp fresh lemon juice
1 small garlic clove, minced
½ tsp finely grated lemon zest (optional)
½ tsp salt
¼ tsp freshly ground black pepper
¼ tsp dry mustard

In a small bowl, whisk together 2 Tbsp of the olive oil, the lemon juice, garlic, lemon zest, salt, pepper, and mustard until emulsified. Whisk in the remaining 1 Tbsp oil if needed to thin to a good consistency.

Sesame Sauce

⅓ cup [50 g] sesame seeds
2 Tbsp sugar
2 tsp soy sauce
1½ tsp mirin
¼ cup [60 ml] warm water

Place a small frying pan over medium heat. Add the sesame seeds and cook, stirring or swirling constantly, until the sesame seeds are just starting to turn a deeper gold. Transfer the toasted sesame seeds to a mortar or a small bowl. Use a pestle or a wooden spoon to work the sesame seeds into a paste. Add the sugar, soy sauce, and mirin and work them into the sesame paste. Stir in the water to thin the paste to a sauce.

Parsley Walnut Pesto

1½ cups [165 g] walnut pieces
2 to 3 garlic cloves
Leaves from 2 bunches flat-leaf parsley
½ cup [120 ml] walnut oil
1 to 2 Tbsp fresh lemon juice or cider vinegar
½ cup [50 g] grated aged pecorino cheese
Salt

In a large frying pan over medium-high heat, toast the walnuts, shaking the pan frequently, until the walnuts start to smell toasty and take on a bit of color, 3 to 5 minutes. Take care not to let them darken too much in the pan, as they will continue to toast when you take them off the heat. Transfer them to a plate or cutting board and let cool.

In a blender or food processor, pulse the garlic until minced, stopping to scrape down the sides as needed. Add the parsley leaves and pulse until they have reduced a bit. Add the walnut oil and lemon juice and whirl until the sauce is fairly smooth. Add the walnuts and pulse until as smooth as you like (I prefer to have some chunks of walnut in the sauce when it is finished). Add the cheese and pulse to combine. Season with salt.

Peanut Sauce

½ cup [130 g] creamy peanut butter
⅓ cup [80 ml] warm water, plus more as needed
2 Tbsp soy sauce
1 Tbsp fresh lime juice
1 Tbsp peeled and finely grated fresh ginger
1 garlic clove, minced
1 teaspoon brown sugar
¼ to ½ tsp red pepper flakes

In a medium bowl, whisk together the peanut butter, water, soy sauce, lime juice, ginger, garlic, brown sugar, and the pepper flakes to taste. (If you like, whirl together all of the ingredients in blender or food processor.) Add more water, 1 Tbsp at a time, until the sauce is as thin and as drizzle-ready as you like.

Raita

1 cup [240 ml] plain whole-milk yogurt
1 small cucumber, peeled, halved lengthwise, seeded, and grated on the large holes of a box grater
Leaves from 6 fresh cilantro sprigs, minced
12 large fresh mint leaves, minced
1 green onion, white and green parts, trimmed and minced
¼ tsp ground coriander
¼ tsp ground cumin
Salt

In a medium bowl, combine the yogurt, cucumber, cilantro, mint, green onion, coriander, and cumin and stir to mix well. Season with salt, then let sit for at least 15 minutes or cover and refrigerate for up to overnight.

Roasted Chile Sauce

2 serrano or jalapeño chiles
1 small garlic clove, minced
3 Tbsp olive oil
1 Tbsp fresh lime juice
¼ tsp salt

You can roast the chiles over a hot fire in a charcoal or gas grill, over the flame of a burner on a gas range, or on a baking sheet under a preheated broiler. Using tongs, turn the chiles as needed until charred and blistered on all sides, then set aside to cool. When the chiles are cool enough to handle, rub off their blackened skin, pull out their stem and seeds, and finely chop them. If properly roasted, they will sort of fall apart as you chop them.

In a bowl, combine the chiles, garlic, olive oil, lime juice, and salt and whisk until the sauce looks creamy. Taste and adjust with more salt if needed.

Romesco

2 red bell peppers
½ cup [55 g] slivered blanched almonds
½ cup [120 ml] olive oil
5 garlic cloves, chopped
3 tomatoes, peeled and chopped
2 árbol or other small dried hot chiles, stemmed, seeded, and chopped
⅓ cup [80 ml] chicken or vegetable broth
3 Tbsp dry white wine
½ tsp fine sea salt
1 Tbsp red wine vinegar

You can roast the bell peppers over a hot fire in a charcoal or gas grill, over the flame of a burner on a gas range, or on a baking sheet under a preheated broiler. Using tongs, turn the peppers as needed until charred and blistered on all sides, then set aside to cool. When the bell peppers are cool enough to handle, rub off their blackened skin, pull out their stem and seeds, and roughly chop. Set the peppers aside.

In a medium saucepan over medium-high heat, toast the almonds, stirring constantly, until they start to brown, about 3 minutes. Pour onto a small plate and set aside.

Return the pan to medium-high heat and add the olive oil. When the oil is hot, add half of the garlic and cook, stirring, until fragrant, about 1 minute. Add the tomatoes, roasted peppers, chiles, broth, wine, and salt and cook, stirring occasionally, until the vegetables are all very soft, about 20 minutes. Remove from the heat and let cool.

In a blender or food processor, combine the cooled tomato-pepper mixture, almonds, the remaining garlic, and the vinegar and whirl until extremely smooth. (Let the machine run for at least 2 minutes.) Taste and add more salt if needed. Serve the sauce warm or at room temperature. It will keep in an airtight container in the refrigerator for up to 3 days.

Rouille

1 red bell pepper
1 egg
1 Tbsp fresh lemon juice, plus more if needed for thinning
1 garlic clove, crushed or minced
½ tsp Dijon mustard
1 small fresh red chile, seeded and finely chopped (optional)
¾ cup [180 ml] extra-virgin olive oil
Salt

You can roast the bell pepper over a hot fire in a charcoal or gas grill, over the flame of a burner on a gas range, or on a baking sheet under a preheated broiler. Using tongs, turn the pepper as needed until charred and blistered on all sides, then set aside to cool. When the pepper is cool enough to handle, rub off the blackened skin and pull out the stem and seeds.

In a blender or food processor, whirl together the egg, lemon juice, garlic, and mustard until blended. Add the roasted pepper and the chile, if using, and whirl until a smooth paste forms. With the motor running on low speed, slowly add the olive oil, a drop or two at a time, allowing each addition to incorporate into the egg mixture before adding more. Once the mixture has emulsified, thickened, and lightened in color, you can begin adding the remaining oil in a slow, steady stream. When all of the oil has been incorporated, season the mixture with salt. If the mixture is too thick, thin with a few drops of lemon juice (although counterintuitive, more oil will thicken the mixture).

This garlicky rust-colored sauce, a classic of Provence where it traditionally accompanies fish soups and other fish dishes, is a good topping for seafood bowls.

Salsa Verde

1 lb [455 g] tomatillos, husks removed and rinsed
1 small onion, quartered
4 serrano or 2 jalapeño chiles
3 garlic cloves, unpeeled
¼ cup [10 g] chopped fresh cilantro
½ tsp sugar
2 Tbsp olive oil
¾ cup [180 ml] chicken or vegetable broth
1 to 2 Tbsp fresh lime juice
Salt

Prepare a fire in a charcoal or gas grill for direct-heat cooking over medium-high heat. (You should be able to hold your hand about 1 in [2.5 cm] above the cooking grate for 3 to 4 seconds before you must pull it away.)

Thread the tomatillos, onion quarters, chiles, and garlic each on their own thin metal skewers. Oil the cooking grate. Set the skewers on the grate directly over the fire and cook, turning as needed, until the vegetables are tender and the skins on the garlic, tomatillos, and chiles are charred, about 10 minutes for the onion, 8 minutes for the tomatillos and chiles, and 5 minutes for the garlic. Let everything sit until cool enough to handle, then remove the charred skins. Remove and discard the stem and seeds from the chiles and core the tomatillos. Transfer the tomatillos, onion, chiles, and garlic to a blender, add the cilantro and sugar, and pulse until a purée forms.

CONT'D

In a large saucepan over medium-high heat, warm the olive oil. When the oil is hot, add the purée and cook, stirring frequently, until it thickens slightly, 2 to 3 minutes. Add the broth and simmer, stirring occasionally, until reduced by about one-third. Remove from the heat, stir in the lime juice to taste, and season with salt. Serve warm or at room temperature.

This recipe makes more than you will need for four bowls, but it stores beautifully for a future bowl-centric meal. Pack it into an airtight container and refrigerate for up to 3 days or freeze for up to 6 months.

Shatta

4 garlic cloves, chopped
4 Fresno or 8 Thai bird chiles, chopped
½ cup [20 g] chopped fresh flat-leaf parsley
½ cup [20 g] chopped fresh cilantro
2 tsp white vinegar
1 tsp olive oil
½ tsp salt
½ tsp freshly ground black pepper
½ tsp ground cumin
⅓ cup [85 g] tomato paste
½ cup [120 ml] warm water

In a blender or food processor, combine the garlic, chiles, parsley, cilantro, vinegar, olive oil, salt, pepper, cumin, tomato paste, and water and whirl until smooth. Taste and adjust with salt if needed.

This Middle Eastern hot sauce packs a punch, so you won't need much for each bowl. Luckily, it keeps nicely in a tightly covered container in the refrigerator for a good long time. You will know it is past its pull date if mold has formed on the surface.

Sichuan Pepper Vinegar Sauce

4 to 8 small dried Chinese or árbol chiles
2 tsp Sichuan peppercorns
¼ cup [60 ml] canola oil
3 Tbsp Chinese black vinegar, or 2 Tbsp rice vinegar and 1 Tbsp balsamic vinegar
2 Tbsp soy sauce
1 Tbsp toasted sesame oil
1 Tbsp sugar
3 garlic cloves, minced

Heat a small frying pan over medium-high heat. When the pan is hot, add the chiles and peppercorns and cook, stirring frequently, until toasted and fragrant, about 3 minutes. Transfer to a mortar and crush with a pestle until flaky (or use a mini food processor or a bowl and a wooden spoon). Transfer to a medium heatproof bowl.

Return the frying pan to medium heat and add the canola oil. When the oil shimmers, immediately pour it over the chile-peppercorn mixture. Let sit until cooled to lukewarm, about 15 minutes. Add the vinegar, soy sauce, sesame oil, sugar, and garlic and stir until the sugar dissolves.

Tomato Paprika Sauce

2 fresh or canned tomatoes, halved and seeded
3 Tbsp extra-virgin olive oil
1 Tbsp red wine vinegar
1 garlic clove, chopped
½ tsp salt
¼ tsp hot or sweet smoked Spanish paprika

In a blender or food processor, whirl together the tomatoes, olive oil, vinegar, garlic, salt, and paprika until smooth. Taste and adjust with salt if needed.

Vietnamese Nuoc Cham

1 serrano or 3 Thai bird chiles, cut into thin rings
1 garlic clove, minced
3 Tbsp palm sugar or brown sugar
5 Tbsp [80 ml] fish sauce
2 Tbsp fresh lime juice
½ cup [120 ml] warm water
½ small carrot, peeled and finely grated (optional)

If you have a mortar and pestle, combine two-thirds of the chile slices, the garlic, and the palm sugar and pound to a paste with the pestle. If you lack a mortar and pestle, combine the same ingredients on a cutting board and, using a sharp knife, mince together to form a paste. Transfer the paste to a small bowl, add the fish sauce, lime juice, and water, and stir to dissolve the sugar. Add the remaining chile slices and stir in the carrot, if you like.

MORE SAUCES
In Part 3, you will discover more versatile and delicious sauces you can use to dress up bowls:

MORE YUMMY SAUCES TO BE FOUND WITH THE BOWL RECIPES:

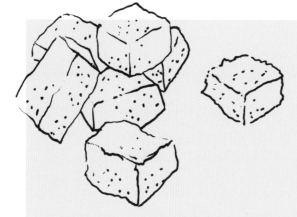

Toppings are where customizing really comes to the fore, and where having a solid pantry on-site will let you turn ho-hum leftovers into beyond-tasty dinners. Most toppings require just a quick chopping or grating, and not always even that: capers, cheeses of all sorts, flowers (nasturtiums) and blossoms (zucchini), fresh herbs, finely grated lemon zest, microgreens, nuts, olives, preserved lemons, seeds of all sorts (chia, sunflower, sesame, poppy, onion), and sprouts from bean to radish.

CREAMY, CRUNCHY, CRISPY TOPPINGS

Crowning a bowl with a creamy finish is even easier. Just a scoop with a spoon will land a dollop of something rich and satisfying on top: burrata cheese, cottage cheese, crème fraîche, marscapone cheese, sour cream, and yogurt.

If you have a little time to put a topping together, here are ten more easy ideas that will complement all kinds of bowls. Each recipe yields enough for four bowls, unless otherwise indicated, and I have included storage information in case you decide to make them in advance. The Frizzled Shallots in the bowl on page 93 would also be delicious strewn over pretty much anything.

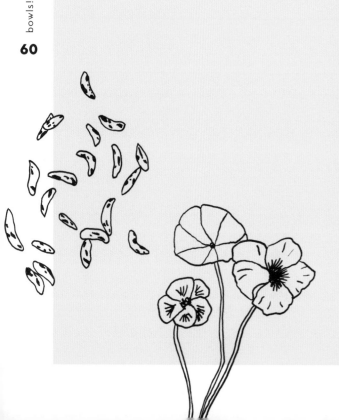

Hand-Torn Croutons

2 cups [100 g] bite-size hand-torn bread pieces
1 Tbsp olive or canola oil or butter, melted

Preheat the oven to 350°F [180°C]. Put the bread pieces in a medium bowl, drizzle with the oil, and toss to coat the pieces as evenly as possible with the oil. Spread the pieces in a single layer on a baking sheet.

Bake the croutons until golden and crunchy, 10 to 15 minutes. Remove from the oven and let cool completely on the pan on a cooling rack. The croutons will crisp up as they cool. Use immediately, or transfer to an airtight container and store at room temperature for up to 2 days.

Use any kind of bread you like. I'm a fan of rye croutons for savory dishes, and cinnamon bread croutons on a breakfast bowl are heavenly.

Buttered Bread Crumbs

1 cup [60 g] fresh bread crumbs
2 Tbsp butter, melted

Preheat the oven to 350°F [180°C]. Put the bread crumbs in a bowl, drizzle with the butter, and toss until the crumbs are evenly coated. Spread them in a single layer (as much as possible) on a baking sheet.

Bake the bread crumbs, stirring them and returning them to a single layer every 5 minutes, until golden brown, about 15 minutes. Remove from the oven and transfer to a plate to cool. Use immediately, or transfer to an airtight container and store at room temperature up to 2 days.

Cumin Pita Crumbles

2 pita breads, torn into bite-size pieces
1 Tbsp olive oil
¼ tsp ground cumin
½ tsp salt

Preheat the oven to 350°F [180°C]. Put the pita pieces in a medium bowl, drizzle with the olive oil, and toss to coat the pieces as evenly as possible with the oil. Sprinkle with the cumin and toss again to distribute evenly. Spread the pita pieces in a single layer on a baking sheet and sprinkle with the salt.

Bake the pita pieces until they just start to turn golden, about 10 minutes. Stir and continue to bake until golden and starting to crisp, about 5 minutes longer. Remove from the oven and let cool completely on the pan on a cooling rack. The pieces will crisp up as they cool. Use immediately, or transfer to an airtight container and store at room temperature for up to 2 days.

Baked Tortilla Strips

4 corn tortillas
Canola or vegetable oil for brushing
Salt

Preheat the oven to 350°F [180°C]. Cut the tortillas into strips of desired size (or into whatever shapes you like). Arrange the strips on a baking sheet. Brush them with oil and sprinkle with salt, then turn them over and brush the second side with oil and sprinkle with salt.

Bake until golden, about 5 minutes. Turn the strips over and continue to bake until golden brown (browning a tad on the edges), about 2 minutes longer (trust your eye over the clock here). Remove from the oven and let cool on the pan on a cooling rack. They will crisp up as they cool. Use immediately, or transfer to an airtight container and store at room temperature for up to 2 days.

Caramelized Nuts

1 cup [145 g] whole natural almonds or [100 g] pecan or walnut halves
1 egg white
¼ cup [50 g] sugar
½ tsp salt
1 tsp cayenne pepper (optional)

Preheat the oven to 325°F [165°C]. Line a baking sheet with parchment paper (it makes cleanup easier). Chop the nuts, if you like. In a medium bowl, whisk the egg white until it is almost watery. Whisk in the sugar and salt and then whisk in the cayenne if you want things spicy. Add the nuts and toss to coat them evenly with the egg white mixture. Spread the coated nuts on the prepared baking sheet in a single layer (as much as possible).

Bake the nuts until browned and crunchy, 10 to 15 minutes. Stir every 5 minutes or so to help the nuts cook evenly. Remove from the oven and transfer to a plate to cool. Use immediately, or transfer to an airtight container and store at room temperature for up to 3 days.

Caramelized Onions

1 Tbsp canola or vegetable oil
1 onion, halved and thinly sliced
¼ tsp salt

In a large frying pan over medium-high heat, warm the oil, swirling the pan to coat the bottom evenly. Add the onion slices, sprinkle with the salt, and cook, stirring frequently, until they are soft and translucent, 3 to 5 minutes. Turn the heat to low and cook, stirring occasionally, until the onions are caramelized, about 20 minutes. Use immediately.

Quick Pickled Red Onions

1 small red onion, halved and thinly sliced
¾ cup [180 ml] distilled white vinegar
½ tsp salt
¼ tsp freshly ground black pepper

In a small bowl, combine the onion, vinegar, salt, and pepper, stirring gently to dissolve the salt. Set aside at room temperature to marinate for at least 30 minutes, or cover and refrigerate for up to 1 week. Drain before adding to bowls.

Homemade Kimchi

One 2-lb [910-g] head napa cabbage
6 cups [1.4 L] water
3 Tbsp salt
6 green onions, white and green parts, chopped or julienned
2 Tbsp peeled and finely grated or minced fresh ginger
2 tsp *gochugaru* (Korean dried red chile flakes), or 2 dried New Mexico chiles, stemmed, seeded, and finely ground

Core the cabbage and then coarsely chop the leaves and transfer to a large bowl. Measure the water into a large pitcher or other similar-size vessel, preferably with a spout. Add the salt and stir to dissolve. Pour this brine over the cabbage, then top the cabbage with a plate or lid to keep it submerged. Let sit at room temperature for about 12 hours.

Drain the cabbage into a colander placed over a bowl to capture the brine. Return the cabbage to the large bowl, add the green onions, ginger, and *gochugaru*, and toss to distribute the seasonings evenly. Stuff this mixture into a sealable container. A large glass jar or pitcher works well; if you have a sauerkraut crock, all the better. Add enough of the reserved brine to cover the mixture.

Place a piece of parchment paper or plastic wrap directly against the surface of the mixture and seal the container. Place the container on a tray or in a larger bowl (to catch any spillage when the cabbage bubbles up as it ferments) and let sit in a cool, dark place for 6 days.

When the kimchi is ready, it should taste sour but spicy and delicious, like a pickle or sauerkraut. (If you see or smell any mold, toss the whole batch.) You can leave it in the same container or transfer it to smaller jars. It will keep in the refrigerator for up to 3 weeks.

Kimchi adds sharp flavor and lots of vitamin C (no joke!) to a bowl and can work as a vegetable or, in smaller amounts, as a garnish. This recipe makes 1 qt [1 L], so it will help add a bright taste to plenty of bowls!

Roasted Garlic Cloves

1 head garlic
Olive oil for drizzling
Salt

Preheat the oven to 350°F [180°C]. Separate the head of garlic into cloves and peel the cloves. Put the cloves in a small baking dish or other ovenproof container (a piece of aluminum foil crimped up at the edges works just fine). Drizzle with a little olive oil, sprinkle with salt, and cover with foil.

Bake the garlic until very tender and evenly browned, about 30 minutes. Remove from the oven and let cool slightly before using. Use immediately, or transfer to an airtight container and store at room temperature for up to 3 days.

Popped Wild Rice

1 tsp canola or vegetable oil
½ cup [90 g] wild rice
Salt

Heat a heavy medium saucepan over medium-high heat. Add the oil and swirl the pan to coat the bottom. When the oil is hot, add the wild rice, cover, and cook, shaking the pan frequently, until the rice "pops." The timing varies greatly. It can range from 3 to 10 minutes, depending on how dry the wild rice is to start. It won't pop as much as popcorn, but the moisture in the rice will turn to steam and force the kernels to pop open. Transfer to a medium bowl and sprinkle with salt. Let cool and use that same day.

Toasted Quinoa

½ cup [90 g] cooked and cooled Quinoa (page 18)
2 tsp canola or vegetable oil

Preheat the oven to 375°F [190°C]. Put the quinoa in a small bowl, drizzle with the oil, and toss to coat the quinoa evenly. Spread the quinoa in a single layer (as much as possible) on a baking sheet.

Bake the quinoa, stirring it and returning it to a single layer every 5 minutes, until browned and toasted, about 25 minutes. Let cool on the pan. Use immediately, or transfer to an airtight container and store at room temperature for up to 3 days.

easy combi- nations

These bowls involve throwing a few things together, as bowls should. Take them as inspiration.

OF A PLACE

ARGENTINE GRILL
Ribboned Kale (page 139), sliced
Steak (page 40), Grilled Vegetables
(page 44), Chimichurri (page 51)

BIBIMBAP BOWL
rice of any sort (pages 15 and 20),
sliced Steak (page 40) or ground
beef (page 38), Homemade Kimchi
(page 63), cilantro, green onions,
sesame seeds, toasted sesame oil, soy
sauce, fried egg (page 27), radish slices

CALIFORNIA ROLL
short-grain brown rice (page 15),
crabmeat, avocado slices, cucumber
slices, crumbled toasted seaweed,
mayonnaise, toasted sesame seeds,
Roasted Chile Sauce (page 55; optional)

SPARTAN JAPANESE
Soba Noodles (page 19), shredded
Baked Tofu (page 29), julienned carrot
and cucumber, sautéed maitake mushrooms, Ginger Vinaigrette (page 52),
toasted sesame seeds, chopped green
onions

LE GRAND AIOLI
steamed potatoes and steamed green
beans (page 44), hard-boiled egg
(page 27), Oil-Poached Tuna (page 33),
cherry tomatoes, Aioli (page 50)

A LITTLE BIT GERMAN BOWL

Quinoa (page 18), black lentils (page 22), sliced sausage or shredded pork (page 40), sautéed red cabbage, whole-grain mustard

NORDIC NIÇOISE

steamed potatoes (page 44) tossed with fresh dill, smoked fish (such as lox or trout), steamed green beans (page 44), chèvre, shredded butter lettuce, Caper Dressing (page 51)

YUCATÁN QUINOA TACO SALAD

Quinoa (page 18) with lime juice, shredded Roast Chicken (page 36) rubbed with achiote before roasting, black beans (page 22), Avocado Vinaigrette (page 50), Salsa Fresca (page 89), shredded cabbage, Quick Pickled Red Onions (page 63)

FRESH + THROWN TOGETHER

SIMPLE SUPPER BOWL

Quinoa (page 18) or short-grain brown rice (page 15), spinach raw or sautéed (page 47), hard-boiled egg (page 27), sprouts, toasted almonds, sweet soy sauce

HUMMUS + SOME

Bulgur (page 16), hummus, avocado slices, Lemon Garlic Vinaigrette (page 54), poached egg (page 26), toasted pine nuts, dried currants

NO-NOODLE BOWL
Spaghetti Squash (page 47), diced tofu (marinated, if you dare, page 31), grated radish, mung bean sprouts, Peanut Sauce (page 55)

SPRIGHTLY FRESH
grain of choice, steamed edamame (page 44), sautéed carrots, Basil Pesto (page 50), chopped peanuts

GREENS, MAGICAL GREENS
Quinoa (page 18), sautéed garlicky broccoli rabe (page 47), fresh herbs, sliced chile, minced raw dandelion greens (just a bit), Green Olive Sauce (page 53), poached egg (page 26)

ROASTED VEGETABLES DELUXE
roasted cauliflower, winter squash, zucchini, kale, and cabbage (page 43); toasted almonds; Creamy Dill Sauce (page 51)

HIPPIE GOODNESS

HIPPIE SOUTHERNER
Polenta (page 18), Baked Tofu with BBQ Marinade (pages 29 and 31), Sautéed Greens (page 47), Pot Likker Beans (page 23)

THE RANDOM HIPPIE
Quinoa (page 18), Lentils (page 22), roasted winter squash (page 43), Quick Pickled Red Onions (page 63), roasted tomatoes (page 43), Rouille (page 56), chopped fresh dill

THE REFINED HIPPIE
white beans (page 22), wilted escarole and radicchio, avocado slices, Feta Vinaigrette (page 52), chopped peanuts, Toasted Quinoa (page 64)

THE SPICY HIPPIE
Lentils (page 22), Brown Rice (page 15), sautéed greens (page 47), Caramelized Onions (page 62), Shatta (page 58)

IT'S BREAKFAST TIME

FALLING LEAVES BREAKFAST
Steel-Cut Oats (page 19), diced apples, spiced caramelized walnuts (page 62), roasted pumpkin seeds

NORTH WOODS BREAKFAST
Wild Rice (page 20), country sausage, dried cranberries, maple or birch syrup, chopped fresh chives, toasted pecans

SPUNKY BREAKFAST
sweet potato hash (page 45), Scrambled Eggs (page 28), sauerkraut, green onions

SIMPLE BREAKFAST (OR HUMBLE DINNER)
sweet brown rice (page 15), fried egg (page 27), crumbled toasted seaweed, Homemade Kimchi (page 63), chile oil

TWISTED LOWCOUNTRY BREAKFAST (LUNCH OR DINNER)
Polenta (page 18), Poached Shrimp (page 35), roasted okra (page 43), crumbled crisp bacon, Romesco (page 56), shredded Cheddar cheese, chopped tomato

MIGHTY MEATY

NEW STEAK HOUSE
short-grain brown rice (page 15), sliced Steak (page 40), roasted broccoli (page 43), *gochujang* (Korean chile sauce), sesame seeds

NORTHERN HUNT
Wild Rice (page 20), sliced or shredded smoked duck, cranberry beans (page 22), braised radicchio, crumbled blue cheese, chopped green onions

OLD-SCHOOL TACO BOWL
pinto beans (page 22), ground beef (page 38) with cumin and cayenne pepper, shredded lettuce, guacamole, Salsa Verde (page 57), shredded Monterey Jack cheese, Baked Tortilla Strips (page 62)

BY THE SEASON

SPRING IS SPRUNG
Quinoa (page 18) with lots of dill and chervil, flaked cooked salmon, steamed asparagus and fiddlehead ferns (if you can find them; page 44), grilled morel mushrooms (page 44), Green Garlic Sauce (page 52)

SUMMER NIGHT SUPPER
shredded lettuce, Grilled Shrimp (page 34), avocado slices, sliced chile, Basil Vinaigrette (page 51)

THANKSGIVING IN A BOWL
Mashed Potatoes (page 46), shredded leftover roasted turkey, roasted Brussels sprouts (page 43), leftover or roasted sweet potatoes (page 43), cranberry sauce

WINTER WARM-UP
Winter Squash Mash (page 48),
Lentils (page 22), roasted mushrooms
(page 43), toasted walnuts, Parsley
Walnut Pesto (page 54)

A BOWL FOR ALL SEASONS
white beans (page 22), wilted escarole
and radicchio, avocado slices, Feta
Vinaigrette (page 52), chopped
peanuts, Toasted Quinoa (page 64)

full
bowls

This is where the rubber hits the road—recipes for bowls designed to go together from the ground up. These recipes, as with the others in this book, are meant to serve four. They all include an Order of Operations designed to give a quick view of how to get all the components of each bowl done in the most efficient

fashion. Some also come with a Make It Easy note that suggests ways to get similar results with less kitchen effort. As with all bowls, feel free to play. Trade out an element for a similar one, mix things up, add more garnishes, use a different sauce, make just one of the subrecipes and call it a day—how you use these recipes is entirely up to you, your taste, and who's at your table.

The Minty Goddess

mint lemon quinoa + falafel-esque chickpeas + cucumber tomato salad +
tahini harissa dressing + olives + feta

ORDER OF OPERATIONS
1. Cook the quinoa
2. Make the chickpeas
3. Make the salad
4. Make the dressing
5. Assemble the bowls

mint lemon quinoa

5 Tbsp [80 ml] olive oil

1 cup [180 g] quinoa

2 cups [480 ml] water

1 garlic clove, chopped

1 tsp finely grated lemon zest

2 Tbsp fresh lemon juice

12 large fresh mint leaves

Salt

falafel-esque chickpeas

2 Tbsp olive oil

1 onion, chopped

½ tsp fine sea salt

2 to 3 garlic cloves, minced

½ tsp ground cumin

One 14½-oz [415-g] can chickpeas, drained
and rinsed, or 1¾ cups [420 g] drained home-
cooked chickpeas

¼ cup [5 g] fresh flat-leaf parsley leaves,
chopped

¼ cup [5 g] fresh cilantro leaves, chopped

2 Tbsp tahini

cucumber tomato salad

1 English or other slicing cucumber, peeled,
halved, seeded, and chopped

2 tomatoes, chopped

tahini harissa dressing

1 Tbsp tahini

1 Tbsp extra-virgin olive oil

1 Tbsp fresh lemon juice

½ tsp Harissa (page 53), or to taste

½ cup [90 g] Kalamata or oil-cured black olives,
pitted and chopped

½ cup [75 g] crumbled feta cheese

FOR THE QUINOA: In a medium saucepan
over medium-high heat, warm 1 Tbsp of the
olive oil. Add the quinoa and cook, stirring
frequently, until toasted, about 3 minutes. Add
the water, bring to a boil, cover, turn the heat
to low, and cook, undisturbed, until the quinoa
is tender and fluffy and the liquid is absorbed,
about 20 minutes. Remove from the heat and
fluff with a fork.

While the quinoa cooks, combine the garlic,
lemon zest and juice, mint, and the remaining
4 Tbsp [60 ml] olive oil in a blender and whirl
until smooth to make a sauce. Season
with salt.

CONT'D

When the quinoa is ready, scoop out 1 Tbsp of the sauce and set aside to use with the salad. Pour the remaining sauce over the quinoa, and toss to combine. Cover and set aside.

FOR THE CHICKPEAS: In a large frying pan over medium-high heat, warm the olive oil. Add the onion and sprinkle with the salt. Cook, stirring occasionally, until the onion is soft, about 3 minutes. Add the garlic (use the larger amount if you favor garlic) and cook, stirring, until fragrant, about 1 minute. Add the cumin and stir to combine while it sizzles. Add the chickpeas and cook, stirring occasionally, until warmed through, about 3 minutes. Stir in the parsley, cilantro, and tahini and cook, stirring, until the herbs are wilted, about 2 minutes. Cover and set aside.

FOR THE SALAD: In a medium bowl, combine the cucumber and tomato and toss to mix. Drizzle with the 1 Tbsp sauce reserved from the quinoa.

FOR THE DRESSING: In a small bowl or measuring cup, whisk together the tahini, olive oil, and lemon juice. Add the harissa, adjusting the amount according to how spicy your version is and how much kick you like.

TO ASSEMBLE: Divide the quinoa among four bowls. Arrange the chickpeas and salad on the quinoa and drizzle with the dressing. Top with the olives and feta and serve.

A Halloumi of a Time

herbed lentils + lemony grilled halloumi + burst tomatoes + shaved zucchini salad

ORDER OF OPERATIONS

1. Marinate the halloumi
2. Cook the lentils
3. Cook the tomatoes
4. Make the salad
5. Grill the halloumi
6. Assemble the bowls

lemony grilled halloumi

1 Tbsp olive oil

1 Tbsp fresh lemon juice

8 oz [230 g] halloumi cheese (brined semihard Cypriot cheese, aka grilling cheese)

herbed lentils

1 cup [200 g] brown lentils, rinsed

Salt

1 small red onion, diced

1 cup [20 g] lightly packed fresh herb leaves, chopped (flat-leaf parsley, cilantro or dill, and a bit of mint and thyme is a nice mix)

1 Tbsp extra-virgin olive oil

Freshly ground black pepper

burst tomatoes

3 Tbsp olive oil

1 pt [300 g] cherry or grape tomatoes

Salt

shaved zucchini salad

1 zucchini

1 lemon

2 Tbsp extra-virgin olive oil

Salt

Leaves from 2 to 3 fresh mint sprigs, chopped (optional)

FOR THE HALLOUMI: In a bowl large enough to hold the halloumi, whisk together the olive oil and lemon juice. Add the halloumi and let sit for about 30 minutes.

Prepare a fire in a charcoal or gas grill for direct-heat cooking over medium heat. (You should be able to hold your hand about 1 in [2.5 cm] above the cooking grate for 4 to 5 seconds before you must pull it away.)

FOR THE LENTILS: While the cheese marinates, put the lentils in a saucepan and add water to cover. Place over high heat, bring to a boil, lower the heat to maintain a steady simmer, and cook until the lentils are al dente (just barely tender to the bite with a bit of resistance in the center); start testing after 15 minutes. Remove from the heat, add enough salt to the water until it tastes salty, and let sit until the lentils are fully tender, about 10 minutes.

CONT'D

While the lentils are sitting, in a medium bowl, combine the onion and herbs. Drain the lentils, add them, still hot, to the bowl, and toss to combine. Drizzle with the olive oil, toss to coat, and season with black pepper. Cover and set aside to keep warm, or let cool off and serve at room temperature.

FOR THE TOMATOES: In a large frying pan over medium heat, warm the olive oil. Add the tomatoes and cook, shaking the pan now and again, until the tomatoes "burst" and release their juices into the oil, about 10 minutes. Remove from the heat and season with salt. Set aside.

FOR THE SALAD: Trim off the ends of the zucchini, then cut in half lengthwise. Cut each half lengthwise into paper-thin, even slices (a mandoline is handy here, but a sharp knife and a steady hand work just as well). Put the slices in a medium bowl. Using a fine-rasp Microplane grater or a zester and holding the lemon over the zucchini, zest half of the lemon. Cut the lemon in half and squeeze the juice from half of the lemon over the zucchini. Drizzle the zucchini with the olive oil, sprinkle with salt, and toss to coat the zucchini evenly. Taste a piece of zucchini and add more lemon juice or salt if you like. Sprinkle with the mint, if desired.

TO GRILL THE HALLOUMI: Oil the cooking grate. Lift the cheese out of the marinade, set it on the grate directly over the fire, and cook until browned on the first side, 3 to 4 minutes. Flip the halloumi and brown on the second side, 3 to 4 minutes longer. Transfer the halloumi to a cutting board and cut into 8 or 12 even slices.

TO ASSEMBLE: Divide the lentils among four bowls. Arrange the halloumi, tomatoes, and zucchini salad in three separate and equal sections on top of the lentils and serve.

MAKE IT EASY: Instead of cooking cherry tomatoes in a frying pan on the stove top, put 4 medium tomatoes on the cooking grate alongside the halloumi and leave them until they soften, about 8 minutes. Or skip firing up the grill and use a frying pan over medium-high on the stove top for grilling the cheese.

Addis Ababa Lane

kasha-style buckwheat + browned onion split peas + turmeric vegetables + shredded romaine salad + farmer cheese

ORDER OF OPERATIONS
1. Start the split peas
2. Cook the vegetables
3. Cook the buckwheat
4. Cook the onion and add to the split peas
5. Make the salad
6. Assemble the bowls

browned onion split peas

1 cup [200 g] yellow split peas or chana dal (split desi-type chickpea), rinsed

4 cups [960 ml] water

1 tsp peeled and grated fresh turmeric, or 2 tsp ground turmeric

1 onion, roughly chopped

3 Tbsp olive oil

2 to 3 garlic cloves, minced

turmeric vegetables

2 Tbsp butter or vegetable oil

1 small onion, chopped

6 garlic cloves, smashed

Salt

1 tsp ground ginger

½ tsp ground turmeric

½ tsp freshly ground black pepper

1 head savoy cabbage, or ½ head green cabbage, cored and cut into bite-size pieces

3 Yukon gold potatoes, peeled and cut into bite-size pieces

3 carrots, peeled and cut into bite-size pieces

2 cups [480 ml] water

kasha-style buckwheat

2 cups [480 ml] water

1 Tbsp butter

¼ tsp salt

1 egg

1 cup [180 g] toasted buckwheat (sometimes labeled "kasha")

shredded romaine salad

1 small head romaine lettuce

3 Tbsp extra-virgin olive oil

1 Tbsp red wine vinegar

1 small shallot, minced

¼ tsp dried oregano

¼ tsp salt

Freshly ground black pepper

¾ cup [180 g] farmer cheese or whole-milk cottage cheese

FOR THE SPLIT PEAS: In a medium saucepan, combine the split peas and water, bring to a boil over high heat, and skim off and discard any foam from the surface. Add the turmeric, lower the heat to maintain a steady simmer, and cook, stirring occasionally, until tender, about 20 minutes. Add more water, ½ cup [120 ml] at a time, if needed to keep the peas covered.

FOR THE VEGETABLES: While the split peas are cooking, in a large frying pan or medium saucepan over medium-high heat, melt the butter. Add the onion, garlic, and ½ tsp salt and cook, stirring frequently, until the onion is soft, about 3 minutes. Add the ginger, turmeric, and pepper and cook, stirring, until fragrant, about 1 minute. Add the cabbage, stir to combine, cover, turn the heat to medium-low, and cook until the cabbage starts to wilt, about 3 minutes. Uncover, stir, re-cover, and cook until completely wilted, about 5 minutes longer. Add the potatoes, carrots, and water, stir well, raise the heat to high and bring to a boil. Lower the heat to a simmer, cover, and cook until the potatoes and carrots are tender, about 15 minutes. If necessary, cook with the cover off to reduce the liquid before serving. Keep warm.

FOR THE KASHA: In a medium saucepan over high heat, bring the water to a boil. Add the butter and salt and remove from the heat. In a medium bowl, whisk the egg until blended. Add the buckwheat and stir to coat it evenly.

Heat a large frying pan (nonstick is great, if you have it; otherwise the heavier the pan, the better) over high heat. When the pan is hot, add the egg-coated buckwheat and cook, stirring constantly and scraping up any bits that cling to the pan, until the buckwheat smells toasty and no egg is visible, about 2 minutes. Add the still-hot water, stir to combine, cover, turn the heat to low, and simmer until the buckwheat is tender and the liquid is absorbed, 15 to 20 minutes.

TO FINISH THE SPLIT PEAS: About 10 minutes before the peas are ready, in a blender or food processor, whirl the onion until puréed. In a large frying pan over medium-high heat, cook the onion purée, stirring frequently, until lightly browned, about 10 minutes. When the split peas are tender, add them (as well as any liquid remaining in the pan) to the onion along with the olive oil and cook, stirring occasionally, until the peas start to break down like pea soup, about 10 minutes. Stir in the garlic and keep warm.

FOR THE SALAD: Remove the core and coarse stems from the romaine head and shred the leaves. In a medium bowl, whisk together the olive oil, vinegar, shallot, oregano, and salt. Season with pepper and taste and adjust the salt if needed. Add the romaine and toss to coat evenly.

TO ASSEMBLE: Divide the kasha among four bowls. Top with the split peas and turmeric vegetables, followed by the salad, and finally the farmer cheese, then serve.

MAKE IT EASY: Use bottled "Italian" dressing on the salad.

Saffron Quinoa Bowl

saffron quinoa + Moroccan-spiced root vegetables + spiced roasted chickpeas + poached egg + preserved lemon gremolata + harissa + dates

ORDER OF OPERATIONS

1. Roast the chickpeas
2. Cook the quinoa
3. Cook the vegetables
4. Make the gremolata
5. Poach the eggs (if using)
6. Assemble the bowls

spiced roasted chickpeas

One 14½-oz [415-g] can chickpeas, drained and rinsed, or 1¾ cups [420 g] drained home-cooked chickpeas

1 tsp olive oil

¼ tsp salt

⅛ tsp ground coriander (optional)

⅛ tsp ground cumin (optional)

⅛ tsp ground turmeric (optional)

⅛ tsp cayenne pepper (optional)

saffron quinoa

2 cups [480 ml] chicken or vegetable broth

¼ tsp saffron threads

1 Tbsp butter

1 shallot, minced

1 cup [180 g] quinoa, rinsed

Moroccan-spiced root vegetables

1 carrot

1 parsnip

1 small-to-medium turnip

1 yellow beet or rutabaga

1 small celery root

2 Tbsp canola or vegetable oil

1 onion, chopped

Salt

2 garlic cloves, minced

1 Tbsp *ras el hanout* (North African spice mix)

1 fresh red hot chile, chopped, or 2 small dried hot chiles, such as árbol (optional)

3 cups [720 ml] chicken or vegetable broth

preserved lemon gremolata

Leaves from 8 fresh mint sprigs

Leaves from 10 large fresh flat-leaf parsley sprigs

Rind from ½ preserved lemon, rinsed and finely chopped

1 garlic clove, minced

¼ tsp freshly ground black pepper

2 Tbsp extra-virgin olive oil

Salt

4 eggs, poached (page 26), optional

4 Medjool dates, pitted and chopped

Harissa (page 53) or other hot sauce for serving

CONT'D

FOR THE CHICKPEAS: Preheat the oven to 375°F [190°C]. Line a baking sheet with parchment paper.

Pat the chickpeas dry on several layers of paper towels. Put the chickpeas in a bowl, drizzle with the olive oil, and toss to coat evenly. Sprinkle on the salt and the coriander, cumin, turmeric, and cayenne, if using. Toss to coat the chickpeas evenly. Spread the chickpeas in a single layer on the prepared baking sheet. Roast the chickpeas until browned and a bit crispy, about 45 minutes. While the chickpeas are roasting, cook the quinoa and the vegetables.

FOR THE QUINOA: In a medium saucepan over medium heat, bring the broth to a simmer, sprinkle in the saffron, and remove from the heat. In a medium saucepan over medium-high heat, melt the butter. Add the shallot and cook, stirring, until it starts to brown, about 5 minutes. Add the quinoa and stir to coat evenly with the butter. Pour in the warm saffron broth, bring to a simmer, cover, turn the heat to low, and cook, undisturbed, until the quinoa is tender and fluffy and the broth is absorbed, about 20 minutes. Uncover, fluff with a fork, and re-cover to keep warm until ready to serve.

FOR THE ROOT VEGETABLES: Peel the carrot, parsnip, turnip, beet, and celery root and cut into small bite-size pieces, though keeping them all about the same size is more important than the actual size. In a large sauté pan or frying pan over medium-high heat, warm the vegetable oil. Add the onion and 1/2 tsp salt and cook, stirring, until the onion is soft, about 3 minutes. Add the garlic and cook,

stirring, until fragrant, about 1 minute. Stir in the ras el hanout and chile (if using) and cook, stirring, until fragrant, about 1 minute. Pour in the broth, add the chopped vegetables, and bring to boil. Lower the heat to a simmer and cook until the vegetables are tender, about 15 minutes.

FOR THE GREMOLATA: On a cutting board, finely chop the mint and parsley. Add the preserved lemon and garlic and continue chopping until all of the ingredients are minced and blended together. Transfer to a small bowl, add the pepper and olive oil, and stir to combine. Season with salt.

TO ASSEMBLE: Divide the quinoa among four bowls. Top the quinoa with the root vegetables (transfer them with a slotted spoon or add some of the flavorful broth to the bowl). Add the chickpeas to one side and a poached egg, if desired, to the other. Put a hefty dollop of gremolata on top. Pass the harissa and dates at the table, for everyone to add to taste.

MAKE IT EASY: Skip the gremolata. It's delicious, but this bowl has lots of flavor without it. You can also use other root vegetable combinations (4 to 5 small-to-medium specimens) that you may have on hand (or appeal to you more), including mixes with potatoes and/or sweet potatoes.

Veggie Burrito Bowl

taqueria-style rice + cilantro pinto beans + salsa fresca + avocado + more

ORDER OF OPERATIONS
1. Soak and cook the beans
2. Cook the rice
3. Make the salsa
4. Prepare the avocado and other toppings
5. Assemble the bowls

cilantro pinto beans

1 lb [455 g] dried pinto beans

1 onion, chopped

4 garlic cloves

1 bay leaf

1 bunch cilantro

Salt

taqueria-style rice

1 large tomato, peeled and puréed

About ¾ cup [180 ml] vegetable broth, or as needed

2 Tbsp olive oil

1 small onion, diced

1 garlic clove, minced

½ tsp salt

1 cup [200 g] jasmine or basmati rice

salsa fresca

2 tomatoes, seeded and chopped

1 fresh green chile, seeded and minced

1 to 2 Tbsp minced red onion

1 Tbsp fresh lime juice or red wine vinegar

¼ tsp salt

1 or 2 avocados, halved, pitted, peeled, and sliced

2 to 4 handfuls shredded romaine lettuce

Sour cream for serving (optional)

Shredded Monterey Jack or other mild cheese for serving

FOR THE BEANS: Put the beans in a large bowl, cover them with plenty of cold water, and let soak overnight. Drain the beans, put in a large pot, and cover with fresh water. Bring to a boil over high heat and skim off and discard any foam from the surface. Add the onion, garlic, and bay leaf. Cut off the leaves from the cilantro bunch and save them for the salsa and for mixing into the rice. Tie together the stems with kitchen string and add to the pot. Lower the heat to maintain a steady simmer and cook the beans until they smell like beans and are just tender to the bit and not mushy. The overall timing will depend on the age of the beans, but you should start testing at about 25 minutes. Remove and discard the bay leaf and season with salt. Keep warm until serving.

CONT'D

FOR THE RICE: While the beans are cooking, cook the rice. Measure the puréed tomato and add broth as needed to total 1¾ cups [420 ml]. In a medium saucepan or frying pan over medium-high heat, warm the olive oil. Add the onion and cook, stirring, until soft, about 3 minutes. Add the garlic and salt, stir to combine, and cook until fragrant, about 1 minute. Add the rice and stir to combine, then pour in the tomato-broth mixture and bring to a boil. Cover, turn the heat to low, and cook for 15 minutes. Remove from the heat and let sit, covered, for 5 minutes. Chop enough of the reserved cilantro leaves to measure ½ cup. Uncover the rice, scatter the cilantro over the top, and stir and toss to mix. Keep warm until serving.

FOR THE SALSA: In a medium bowl, combine the tomatoes, chile, and red onion and toss to mix well. Drizzle the lime juice over the top and toss again to mix evenly. If desired, chop enough of the reserved cilantro leaves to measure ⅓ cup [10 g], add to the bowl, and toss to mix. Season with the salt, then taste and adjust with more salt if needed.

TO ASSEMBLE: Divide the rice among four bowls. Top the bowls evenly with the pinto beans, transferring them from their pan to the bowls with a slotted spoon (you want some, but not too much, of the bean liquid to add its flavor to the bowl). Top each bowl with the avocado and lettuce to taste, a dollop of sour cream (if using), the salsa, a scattering of cheese, and any remaining cilantro.

MAKE IT EASY: Rinsed and drained canned beans, simply heated up, as well as store-bought salsa make quick work of this bowl.

Bread-Free Leblebi

seeded bulgur pilaf + soupy chickpeas + wilted frisée + toasted cumin +
poached egg + harissa

ORDER OF OPERATIONS

1. Cook the pilaf
2. Cook the chickpeas
3. Wilt the frisée
4. Poach the eggs
5. Assemble the bowls

seeded bulgur pilaf

1 Tbsp canola or vegetable oil

½ tsp cumin seeds

½ tsp yellow or brown mustard seeds

½ tsp nigella seeds

½ tsp sesame seeds

1 small onion, finely chopped

½ tsp salt

1 cup [140 g] bulgur

1½ cups [360 ml] chicken or vegetable broth

soupy chickpeas

1 tsp olive oil

1 garlic clove, minced

1 large dried red chile (optional)

1 cup [240 ml] chicken or vegetable broth

One 14½-oz [415-g] can chickpeas, rinsed and
drained, or 1¾ cups [420 g] drained home-
cooked chickpeas

wilted frisée

1 Tbsp chopped dates or whole dried currants

1 Tbsp sherry vinegar

1 Tbsp pine nuts

1 tsp olive oil

1 head frisée, chopped

4 to 8 eggs (1 or 2 per serving), poached
(page 26)

2 tsp cumin seeds, toasted in a small dry pan
until fragrant

Harissa (page 53) or other hot sauce
for serving

FOR THE PILAF: Heat a large frying pan over
medium-high heat. When the pan is hot, add
the oil and the cumin, mustard, nigella, and
sesame seeds, cover, and cook until you hear
the seeds pop, about 1 minute. Add the onion
and salt, stir to combine everything, and cook,
stirring occasionally, until the onion starts
to brown, about 5 minutes. Add the bulgur,
stir to combine, and then add the broth. Bring
to a boil, cover, turn the heat to low, and
cook until the liquid is absorbed and bulgur
is tender, 15 to 20 minutes. While the pilaf is
cooking, prepare the chickpeas and frisée.

CONT'D

FOR THE CHICKPEAS: In a medium sauce-pan over medium-high heat, combine the olive oil, garlic, and chile (if using) and cook, stirring, until the garlic starts to turn golden, about 1 minute. Add the broth and chickpeas, bring to a simmer, adjust the heat to maintain a gentle simmer, and let cook until ready to serve.

FOR THE FRISÉE: Put the dates in a small bowl, sprinkle with the vinegar, and set aside. Heat a large frying pan over medium-high heat, add the pine nuts and toast, shaking the pan frequently, until the nuts are lightly browned, about 3 minutes. Transfer to a small bowl or cup. Return the pan to medium-high heat, add the olive oil, and swirl the pan to coat the bottom. Add the frisée and cook, stirring frequently, until wilted, 3 to 5 minutes. Remove from the heat and stir in the pine nuts and dates.

TO ASSEMBLE: Divide the bulgur among four bowls. Top with the chickpeas and the frisée. Add an egg or two to each bowl, sprinkle with the cumin seeds, and serve immediately. Pass the harissa at the table.

Black Pepper Tofu Bowl

gingered coconut brown rice + black pepper tofu + lemongrass roasted broccoli + carrot daikon slaw + frizzled shallots

ORDER OF OPERATIONS

1. Cook the rice
2. Make the slaw
3. Roast the broccoli
4. Fry the shallots
5. Cook the tofu
6. Assemble the bowls

gingered coconut brown rice

1-in [2.5-cm] piece fresh ginger, peeled

1 cup [200 g] brown jasmine rice

One 14-oz [420-ml] can unsweetened coconut milk

¾ cup [180 ml] water

¼ tsp salt

carrot daikon slaw

½ large carrot, peeled and grated

½ large daikon, peeled and grated

1 Tbsp sugar

½ tsp salt

3 Tbsp rice vinegar

lemongrass roasted broccoli

1 lemongrass stalk, lower bulb portion only, tough outer leaves removed and minced

2 Tbsp fish sauce

2 Tbsp brown sugar

1 garlic clove, minced

1 fresh Thai chile, seeded and minced

1 Tbsp canola or vegetable oil

1 bunch broccoli, about 1¼ lb [570 g], cut into bite-size florets

frizzled shallots

½ cup [120 ml] canola, peanut, or vegetable oil

2 shallots, thinly sliced

black pepper tofu

¼ cup [60 ml] fish sauce

2 Tbsp brown sugar

1 Tbsp freshly ground black pepper

1 Tbsp canola, peanut, or vegetable oil

1 lb [455 g] block tofu, cut into bite-size pieces

½ cup [120 ml] water

CONT'D

FOR THE RICE: Using the flat side of a cleaver or other large knife or a meat mallet, smash the ginger. In a medium saucepan, combine the ginger (and any juices you can capture), rice, coconut milk, water, and salt, stir to combine, and bring to a boil over high heat, stirring frequently. Turn the heat to low, cover, and cook until the liquid is absorbed and the rice is tender, about 45 minutes. Remove the pan from the heat and let sit, covered, for 10 minutes.

FOR THE SLAW: Combine the carrot and daikon in a large bowl. Sprinkle with the sugar and salt, stir and toss to combine, and then pour in the vinegar. Stir again to mix well, pushing the vegetables under the liquid. Let sit for at least 30 minutes (or cover and chill for up to 1 week). Drain and squeeze dry before serving.

FOR THE ROASTED BROCCOLI: Preheat the oven to 375°F [190°C]. In a large bowl, combine the lemongrass, fish sauce, brown sugar, garlic, chile, and oil and stir to dissolve the sugar. Add the broccoli and toss to coat evenly with the marinade. Spread the broccoli in a single layer in a roasting pan or baking sheet. Roast until browned and tender, about 20 minutes.

FOR THE SHALLOTS: Line a plate with a few layers of paper towels. In a wide medium saucepan over medium-high heat, warm the oil until a shallot slice dropped into the hot oil sizzles on contact and browns in 1 to 2 minutes without burning. Add the shallots and let them sizzle and bob in the oil, stirring a bit to keep them from clumping, until browned, 5 to 8 minutes. Using a slotted spoon, transfer them to the towel-lined plate to drain. Pour off all but 1 Tbsp of the oil (discard the oil or reserve this shallot-infused oil for another use) and use the same pan and the oil for the tofu.

FOR THE TOFU: In a small bowl, combine the fish sauce, brown sugar, and black pepper and stir to dissolve the sugar. Return the pan used for the shallots to medium-high heat. When the pan is hot, add the sauce mixture. It should sizzle immediately. Add the tofu, stir to coat with the sauce, and pour in the water. Bring to a boil and cook, stirring frequently, until the liquid reduces by about one-quarter, about 5 minutes.

TO ASSEMBLE: Divide the rice among four bowls. Top with the tofu, including some of the sauce, and the broccoli. Add the slaw, garnish with the shallots, and serve.

Spanish Shrimp

red lentil quinoa pilaf + smoked paprika shrimp + escarole salad + corn

ORDER OF OPERATIONS
1. Cook the pilaf
2. Make the salad
3. Cut corn kernels from cob(s)
4. Cook the shrimp
5. Assemble the bowls

red lentil quinoa pilaf

2 Tbsp olive oil

1 cup [180 g] quinoa

¼ cup [30 g] pine nuts

2 garlic cloves, minced

¼ tsp red pepper flakes (optional)

½ cup [105 g] red lentils, rinsed

2 cups [480 ml] chicken broth

escarole salad

1 tsp cumin seeds

1 garlic clove, minced

1 Tbsp sherry vinegar

3 Tbsp extra-virgin olive oil

Salt and freshly ground black pepper

1 head escarole, cored and torn into bite-size pieces

smoked paprika shrimp

1 garlic clove, minced

1 tsp hot paprika

1 tsp smoked paprika

½ tsp salt

1 lb [455 g] peeled and deveined shrimp

1 Tbsp olive oil

Kernels from 1 (or 2!) ear corn for garnish

FOR THE PILAF: In a medium saucepan over medium-high heat, combine the olive oil, quinoa, and pine nuts and stir until the quinoa and pine nuts are lightly toasted, about 3 minutes. Add the garlic and pepper flakes (if using) and continue stirring until fragrant, about 1 minute. Add the lentils and the broth and bring to a boil. Cover, turn the heat to low, and cook until the liquid is absorbed and the quinoa and lentils are tender, about 20 minutes. Uncover and fluff with a fork. Serve hot, warm, or at room temperature.

FOR THE SALAD: Heat a small frying pan over high heat. When the pan is hot, add the cumin seeds and cook, shaking the pan constantly, until toasted, about 1 minute. Transfer the cumin seeds to a mortar, let them cool slightly, and crush them with a pestle (or put them on a cutting board and crush them with a meat mallet or the bottom of a small, heavy frying pan).

CONT'D

Put the crushed cumin seeds, garlic, vinegar, and olive oil in a large bowl. Whisk to combine, then season with salt and pepper. Add the escarole and toss to coat evenly. Set aside.

FOR THE SHRIMP: In a medium bowl, stir together the garlic, hot and smoked paprika, and salt. Add the shrimp and toss to coat evenly with the spices. Let sit for 5 to 10 minutes. Heat a large frying pan over medium-high heat and add the olive oil. When the oil is hot, add the shrimp and cook, turning once, until they are pink and opaque, about 2 minutes. Remove from the heat.

TO ASSEMBLE: Divide the pilaf among four bowls. Arrange the shrimp on top of one side of the pilaf and the escarole on top of the other side. Scatter the corn kernels over all and serve.

Mussels Matter

garlicky green quinoa + marinated mussels + tomato confit + butter lettuce + buttered bread crumbs

ORDER OF OPERATIONS
1. Make the tomato confit
2. Cook and marinate the mussels
3. Cook the quinoa
4. Toast the bread crumbs
5. Assemble the bowls

tomato confit

8 tomatoes

½ cup [120 ml] olive oil

3 garlic cloves

3 fresh thyme sprigs

½ tsp salt

marinated mussels

1 small onion, chopped

1 cup [240 ml] dry white wine

1 cup [240 ml] water

2 lb [910 g] small mussels, scrubbed and debearded

2 Tbsp fresh lemon juice

1 Tbsp chopped fresh flat-leaf parsley

2 tsp extra-virgin olive oil

1 tsp drained capers, rinsed

¼ tsp dry mustard

¼ tsp freshly ground black pepper

1 celery stalk, minced

garlicky green quinoa

1 Tbsp olive oil

1 shallot, minced

3 garlic cloves, minced

1 cup [30 g] packed spinach leaves, chopped

1 cup [180 g] white quinoa, rinsed

2 cups [480 ml] chicken or vegetable broth

¼ cup [10 g] minced fresh flat-leaf parsley

8 fresh chives, minced

4 large butter lettuce leaves, torn into bite-size pieces

¼ cup [30 g] Buttered Bread Crumbs (page 61)

FOR THE CONFIT: Preheat the oven to 325°F [165°C]. Cram the tomatoes into an 8-inch [20-cm] square baking dish. Pour the olive oil over them. Tuck the garlic cloves and thyme sprigs in among the tomatoes and sprinkle the tomatoes evenly with the salt. Bake for 1 hour, spooning the oil in the dish over the tomatoes a few times if you think of it. Lower the heat to 250°F [120°C] and continue to cook until the tomatoes collapse, about 1 hour longer.

CONT'D

FOR THE MUSSELS: Put the onion, wine, and water in a large pot and bring to a boil over high heat. Lower the heat to maintain a simmer and cook until the liquid is reduced by half. Add the mussels (discarding any that fail to close to the touch), cover, and cook until they open, 3 to 5 minutes. Using a slotted spoon, lift the mussels out of the pot and transfer to a large bowl. Let sit until cool enough to handle, then remove the mussels from their shells (discard any mussels that haven't opened). Discard the shells and the cooking liquid.

In a medium bowl, combine the lemon juice, parsley, olive oil, capers, mustard, and pepper and mix well. Add the mussels and toss to coat evenly. Add the celery and toss again. Let sit for at least 5 minutes or up to 20 minutes.

FOR THE QUINOA: In a medium saucepan or a large frying pan over medium-high heat, warm the olive oil. Add the shallot and cook, stirring frequently, until soft, about 3 minutes. Add the garlic and cook, stirring often, until fragrant, about 1 minute. Add the spinach and cook until the leaves wilt and the liquid they give off evaporates. Add the quinoa and stir to combine. Pour in the broth, bring to a boil, cover, turn the heat to low, and cook, undisturbed, until the quinoa is tender and fluffy and the liquid is absorbed, about 20 minutes. Uncover, fluff with a fork, and stir in the parsley and chives.

TO ASSEMBLE: Divide the quinoa among four bowls. Arrange the mussels and tomatoes side by side on the quinoa. Garnish with the lettuce and bread crumbs and serve.

MAKE IT EASY: If the long-cooking confit isn't on your agenda, simple chopped fresh tomatoes are pretty darn tasty here, too.

Inca Bowl

spiced roasted sweet potatoes + ceviche + leche de tigre + chopped cilantro salad + microgreens + Peruvian corn nuts + ají chile

ORDER OF OPERATIONS

1. Roast the sweet potatoes
2. Make the leche de tigre
3. Make the ceviche
4. Make the salad
5. Assemble the bowls

spiced roasted sweet potatoes

3 large sweet potatoes, peeled and cut into bite-size cubes

1 Tbsp canola or vegetable oil

½ tsp ground red chile

leche de tigre

⅔ cup [160 ml] fresh lime juice

¼ cup [60 ml] water

2 garlic cloves, chopped

½ ají or habanero chile, seeded

ceviche

1½ lb [680 g] fish fillet, peeled and deveined shrimp, sea scallops, and/or cleaned calamari, cut into bite-size pieces

chopped cilantro salad

1 small red onion, chopped

1 bunch cilantro, chopped

4 celery stalks, chopped

2 Tbsp olive oil

Salt

2 oz [55 g] microgreens or sprouts

2 oz [55 g] *quicos* (Peruvian corn nuts)

1 ají or habanero chile, stemmed, seeded, and sliced into thin rings

FOR THE SWEET POTATOES: Preheat the oven to 400°F [200°C]. Spread the sweet potatoes in a single layer on a baking sheet. Drizzle with the oil and toss to coat evenly. Sprinkle with the ground chile and toss to distribute as evenly as possible. Spread the potatoes again into a single layer. Roast, turning the cubes as needed, until tender and browned on all sides, about 45 minutes.

FOR THE LECHE DE TIGRE: In a blender, whirl together the lime juice, water, garlic, and chile until smooth. Measure out 2 tsp to use for the salad. Reserve the remainder, about ¾ cup [180 ml], for the ceviche.

CONT'D

FOR THE CEVICHE: In a medium bowl, combine the fish and/or seafood and the reserved leche de tigre, stir gently to mix well, cover, and refrigerate for about 15 minutes.

FOR THE SALAD: In a medium bowl, toss together the onion, cilantro, and celery. Drizzle with the olive oil and the reserved 2 tsp leche de tigre and toss to coat the salad evenly. Season with salt.

TO ASSEMBLE: Divide the sweet potatoes among four bowls. Top with the ceviche (use a slotted spoon to transfer to the bowls) and spoon the salad alongside the ceviche. Garnish with the microgreens and corn nuts and serve. Pass the chile at the table, for diners to add more if they dare.

Sweet and Crunchy Salmon

Swiss chard–barley pilaf + maple-glazed salmon + fennel green apple salad + chickpeas + pecans

ORDER OF OPERATIONS

1. Cook the pilaf
2. Roast the salmon
3. Make the fennel salad
4. Assemble the bowls

Swiss chard–barley pilaf

1 bunch Swiss chard

2 Tbsp butter

6 green onions, white and green parts, finely chopped

1 cup [200 g] pearled barley, rinsed

3 cups [720 ml] chicken or vegetable broth

maple-glazed salmon

One 12-oz [340-g] salmon fillet

1 Tbsp maple syrup

1 Tbsp Dijon mustard

⅛ tsp salt

fennel green apple salad

1 bulb fennel

1 small green apple

1 tsp fresh lemon juice

Salt

Freshly ground black pepper (optional)

1 cup [240 g] drained and rinsed canned chickpeas or drained home-cooked chickpeas (page 22)

Chopped fresh dill or flat-leaf parsley for garnish

⅓ cup [40 g] pecans, toasted and chopped

FOR THE PILAF: Preheat the oven to 375°F [190°C]. Cut the stems off of the chard leaves. Finely chop the stems and the leaves, keeping them separate. In a frying pan over medium-high heat, melt the butter. Add the green onions and chard stems and cook, stirring occasionally, until softened, about 3 minutes. Add the barley and stir to mix. Pour in the broth, bring to a boil, cover, turn the heat to low, and cook for 25 minutes. Uncover, scatter the chard leaves over the top (don't stir!), re-cover, and continue cooking over low heat until the leaves are cooked and the barley is tender, about 10 minutes longer. Uncover, stir the chard leaves into the barley, and allow any excess liquid to cook off.

FOR THE SALMON: Place the fillet in a baking dish just large enough to accommodate it. In a small bowl, whisk together the maple syrup, mustard, and salt until blended. Brush or spread the syrup mixture on top of the salmon. Roast the salmon until the glaze is browned and the fish is just cooked through, 10 to 15 minutes; the timing will depend on the thickness of the fillet.

CONT'D

FOR THE SALAD: Trim away the core and any stalks from the fennel, then cut the bulb lengthwise into quarters. Halve and core the apple. Using a mandoline or a sharp knife, cut the fennel quarters into thin slices and then cut the apple halves into thin slices. Stack a few of the apple slices at a time and cut into thin sticks. Put the fennel and apple pieces in a bowl, drizzle with the lemon juice, and toss to combine. Season with salt and pepper.

TO ASSEMBLE: Divide the pilaf among four bowls. Cut the salmon into four pieces. Place one piece in each bowl, or flake each piece and add to the bowl. Pile the salad and chick-peas around the salmon. Garnish with the dill and pecans and serve.

Tuna on Toasted Quinoa

toasted quinoa pilaf + tuna + steamed beets with their greens + cannellini beans + hard-boiled eggs + mustard vinaigrette + olives + radishes

ORDER OF OPERATIONS

1. Hard-boil the eggs for topping
2. Cook the quinoa
3. Steam the beets
4. Make the dressing
5. Assemble the bowls

toasted quinoa pilaf

2 Tbsp butter

1 cup [180 g] quinoa

2 cups [480 ml] chicken or vegetable broth

steamed beets with their greens

1 bunch baby beets with greens attached

1/2 tsp finely grated orange zest

1 tsp fresh orange juice

1/4 tsp salt

mustard vinaigrette

5 Tbsp [80 ml] canola or vegetable oil

2 Tbsp cider vinegar

1 Tbsp Dijon mustard

1/2 tsp honey or maple syrup

Salt and freshly ground black pepper

and more

One 5-oz [140-g] can olive oil-packed tuna, drained

One 14½-oz [415-g] can cannellini beans, rinsed and drained, or 1¾ cups [420 g] drained home-cooked white beans (page 22)

2 to 4 Hard-Boiled Eggs (page 27), peeled and quartered lengthwise

8 to 12 green olives, pitted and chopped

8 radishes, cut into little wedges

FOR THE QUINOA: In a large frying pan over medium-high heat, melt the butter. Add the quinoa and cook, stirring frequently, until it is toasted and browned, 3 to 5 minutes. Pour in the broth, bring to a boil, cover, turn the heat to low, and cook, undisturbed, until the quinoa is tender and fluffy and the liquid is absorbed, about 20 minutes. Uncover and fluff with a fork.

CONT'D

FOR THE BEETS: Cut off the greens and chop them into bite-size pieces. Peel and dice the beets. Select a pot in which a steamer basket or colander will fit. Pour water into the pot to a depth of 1 in [2.5 cm] and bring to a boil over high heat. Put the beets in the basket or colander, set it over the boiling water, cover, and cook until almost tender, about 5 minutes. Strew the chopped greens on top of the beets, re-cover, and cook until the greens are wilted and the beets are fully tender, about 5 minutes longer. Transfer the beets and greens to a bowl, add the orange zest and juice and salt, and toss to coat evenly.

FOR THE VINAIGRETTE: In a small bowl, whisk together the oil, vinegar, mustard, and maple syrup. Season with salt and pepper.

TO ASSEMBLE: Divide the quinoa among four bowls. Arrange the tuna, beets and greens, and beans in three separate and equal sections on top of the quinoa. Top with the eggs, drizzle on the vinaigrette, garnish with the olives and radishes, and serve.

Summer in a Bowl

spicy sautéed corn + yogurt-marinated chicken + ezme salad + tzatziki

ORDER OF OPERATIONS

1. Marinate the chicken
2. Make the tzatziki
3. Make the salad
4. Cook the corn
5. Grill the chicken
6. Assemble the bowls

yogurt-marinated chicken

1 garlic clove, sliced

2 Tbsp plain whole-milk yogurt

1 Tbsp fresh lemon juice

¼ tsp salt

Freshly ground black pepper

1½ lb [680 g] boneless, skinless chicken (preferably thighs), cut into bite-size pieces

tzatziki

1 large English or other slicing cucumber

¾ cup [180 ml] plain yogurt (preferably whole milk)

1 Tbsp extra-virgin olive oil

1 tsp red wine vinegar

1 garlic clove, minced

Salt and freshly ground black pepper

2 Tbsp finely chopped fresh dill (optional)

ezme salad

½ cup [60 g] walnut pieces

3 Tbsp extra-virgin olive oil

1 Tbsp red wine vinegar or cider vinegar

½ tsp salt

2 sweet red bell peppers, seeded and finely chopped

2 tomatoes, seeded and finely chopped

1 shallot, minced

1 garlic clove, minced

½ cup [10 g] fresh flat-leaf parsley leaves, minced

½ tsp red pepper flakes (optional)

spicy sautéed corn

6 ears corn

1 Tbsp vegetable oil

½ tsp brown or yellow mustard seeds

⅛ tsp fenugreek seeds

2 serrano chiles, thinly sliced

¼ tsp ground turmeric (optional)

Salt

¼ cup [10 g] chopped fresh cilantro (optional)

Fresh basil leaves, torn into pieces, for garnish

TO MARINATE THE CHICKEN: In a medium bowl, whisk together the garlic, yogurt, lemon juice, salt, and pepper to taste. Add the chicken to the yogurt mixture, turn to coat evenly, cover, and refrigerate for at least 30 minutes or up to overnight.

About 30 minutes before serving, ready the grill to cook the chicken. Prepare a fire in a charcoal or gas grill for direct-heat cooking over medium-high heat. (You should be able to hold your hand about 1 in [2.5 cm] above the cooking grate for 3 to 4 seconds before you must pull it away.) If using bamboo skewers rather than metal skewers, be sure to soak them in water for about 30 minutes before threading the chicken onto them.

FOR THE TZATZIKI: Peel the cucumber, halve lengthwise, and scoop out any seeds. Using the large holes of a box grater, shred the cucumber into a large bowl. For a less watery salad, sprinkle the cucumber with some salt, let sit for about 20 minutes, then drain the cucumber, squeezing the shreds to release any excess liquid, and transfer to a dry bowl. Stir in the yogurt, olive oil, vinegar, and garlic. Season with salt and pepper and stir in the dill, if using.

FOR THE SALAD: Put the walnuts between two pieces of parchment paper or in a plastic bag and use a rolling pin to crush finely. (Alternatively, pulse them in a food processor, being careful not to turn them into a paste.) In a medium bowl, stir together the olive oil, vinegar, and salt. Add the bell peppers, tomatoes, shallot, and garlic and toss and stir to mix well. Add the parsley, toss again, and stir in the walnuts. If you like things spicy, stir in the pepper flakes.

FOR THE CORN: To remove the kernels from the corn ears, one at a time, stand each ear on its stem end in a wide, shallow bowl. Using a large, sharp knife, slice down the length of the ear, rotating the ear after each cut.

In a large frying pan over medium-high heat, warm the vegetable oil. When the oil is hot, add the mustard and fenugreek seeds, cover, and cook until you hear the seeds pop, about 1 minute. Add the chiles and cook, stirring constantly, until fragrant, about 30 seconds. Stir in the turmeric and then the corn kernels and cook, stirring constantly, until the corn is well mixed with the spices. Cover, turn the heat to low, and cook until the corn is tender to the bite, about 5 minutes. Uncover, increase the heat to high, and cook, stirring occasionally and scraping any browned bits from the bottom of the pan, until the corn starts to brown. Season with salt and stir in the cilantro, if using. Keep warm.

TO GRILL THE CHICKEN: Thread the chicken pieces (let the marinade cling to them) onto skewers. Oil the cooking grate. Set the skewers on the grate directly over the fire and cook, turning once, until browned and cooked through, 4 to 5 minutes per side.

TO ASSEMBLE: Divide the corn among four bowls. Slide the chicken off the skewers and add it to the bowls. Dollop on the tzatziki and the salad, garnish with the basil, and serve.

MAKE IT EASY: Skip firing up the grill and instead cook the chicken on a stove-top grill pan over medium-high heat or under a preheated broiler about 4 in [10 cm] from the heating element. The same timing will work.

Kalefornia Bowl

sautéed white beans + cabbage kale slaw + roast chicken + avocado + serrano chile vinaigrette + peanuts

ORDER OF OPERATIONS
1. Make the vinaigrette
2. Make the slaw
3. Cook the beans
4. Shred the chicken
5. Slice the avocado and chop the peanuts
6. Assemble the bowls

serrano chile vinaigrette

1 serrano chile, seeded and chopped

1 garlic clove, chopped

6 Tbsp [90 ml] vegetable oil

2 Tbsp fresh lime juice

Salt and freshly ground black pepper

cabbage kale slaw

1 bunch Tuscan kale

¼ head savoy cabbage

sautéed white beans

2 Tbsp olive oil

2 garlic cloves, minced

1 fresh rosemary sprig

One 14½-oz [415-g] can white beans, rinsed and drained, or 1¾ cups [420 g] drained home-cooked white beans (page 22)

Salt and freshly ground pepper

2 to 3 cups [220 to 330 g] shredded cooked chicken, from a home-roasted bird (page 36) or purchased rotisserie bird

1 avocado, halved, pitted, peeled, and sliced

⅓ cup [40 g] roasted peanuts, finely chopped

FOR THE VINAIGRETTE: In a blender, whirl together the chile, garlic, vegetable oil, and lime juice until smooth. Season with salt and pepper.

FOR THE SLAW: Trim the thick stems from the kale and core the cabbage. Cut the kale and cabbage into ribbons as finely as possible. Put the ribbons in a large bowl and squeeze them by the handful, "massaging" them to soften their texture a bit. Add about half of the vinaigrette, toss to combine, and let sit for about 10 minutes.

FOR THE BEANS: In a large frying pan over medium-high heat, warm the olive oil, swirling the pan to coat the bottom. Add the garlic and cook, stirring constantly, until just starting to turn golden, about 1 minute. Add the rosemary and beans and cook, stirring, until beans are heated through and some brown bits form, 3 to 5 minutes. Remove and discard the rosemary and season the beans with salt and pepper.

TO ASSEMBLE: Divide the beans among four bowls. Top with the slaw and arrange the chicken and avocado on the slaw. Drizzle with the remaining vinaigrette, sprinkle with the peanuts, and serve.

NOTE: If the chile vinaigrette sounds too spicy for your palate, use Lemon Garlic Vinaigrette (page 54) or Peanut Sauce (page 55).

Nutty Chicken Mushroom Bowl

nutted farro + shredded chicken + marinated mushrooms + lemony carrots + sugar snap peas + avocado + feta

ORDER OF OPERATIONS
1. Marinate the mushrooms
2. Cook the farro
3. Cook the carrots
4. Prep the chicken, peas, avocado, and cheese
5. Assemble the bowls

marinated mushrooms

8 oz [230 g] button or cremini mushrooms

1 tsp fennel seeds

5 Tbsp [80 ml] extra-virgin olive oil

3 Tbsp white wine vinegar

½ tsp salt

¼ tsp freshly ground black pepper

nutted farro

2 Tbsp extra-virgin olive oil

1 onion, finely chopped

½ tsp salt

1 cup [120 g] mixed nuts (almonds, pistachios, walnuts, and pine nuts)

3 garlic cloves, minced

1 tsp ground coriander

½ tsp ground cumin

½ tsp freshly ground black pepper

1 cup [180 g] semipearled or whole-grain farro

1 cup [240 ml] dry white wine

2½ cups [600 ml] vegetable or chicken broth

lemony carrots

1 Tbsp butter

6 carrots, peeled and cut into coins

¼ cup [60 ml] water

1 tsp fresh lemon juice

½ tsp finely grated lemon zest

Salt

2 cups [220 g] shredded cooked chicken, from a home-roasted bird (page 36) or purchased rotisserie bird

6 oz [170 g] sugar snap peas, cut into bite-size pieces

1 avocado, halved, pitted, peeled, and sliced

⅓ cup [50 g] crumbled feta cheese

FOR THE MUSHROOMS: Trim off the stem ends from the mushrooms, then halve or quarter the mushrooms if large. You want the pieces truly bite size. Put the fennel seeds in a mortar and gently crush them with a pestle (or put them on a cutting board and crush them with a meat mallet or the bottom of a small, heavy frying pan).

CONT'D

In a large glass jar or a medium bowl, combine the olive oil, vinegar, fennel seeds, salt, and pepper. If using a jar, screw on the lid and give the jar a few good shakes to combine everything. If using a bowl, whisk everything together. Add the mushrooms, cover, and shake the jar, or stir to coat with the marinade in the bowl. Let the mushrooms sit for at least 30 minutes, shaking or stirring them every 10 minutes or so to recoat them with the marinade. They can be served after 30 minutes or can be refrigerated for up to 3 days before serving.

FOR THE FARRO: In a large frying pan with a tight-fitting lid, combine the olive oil, onion, and salt over medium heat and cook, stirring occasionally, until the onion is soft, about 3 minutes. Increase the heat to high, add the nuts, and cook, stirring constantly, until the nuts start to toast. The onion may brown a bit, which is fine, but lower the heat if it starts to char at all. Add the garlic and cook, stirring, until fragrant, about 30 seconds. Add the coriander, cumin, and pepper and cook, stirring, until the spices are fragrant, about 30 seconds. Add the farro and stir to combine. Pour in the wine and cook, stirring, until absorbed, about 2 minutes. Pour in the broth and bring to a boil. Cover, turn the heat to low, and cook until the farro is tender to the bite, about 20 minutes for semipearled farro and up to 50 minutes for whole-grain farro.

FOR THE CARROTS: In a large frying pan over medium-high heat, melt the butter. Add the carrots and stir to coat with the butter. Add the water, cover, and cook until the carrots are tender, about 5 minutes. Uncover and cook until the liquid has evaporated. Remove from the heat, add the lemon juice and zest, and stir to mix. Season with salt.

TO ASSEMBLE: Divide the farro among four bowls. Arrange the chicken, mushrooms (lift out of the marinade with a slotted spoon), and carrots in three separate and equal sections on top of the farro. Top with the snap peas and avocado. Drizzle on a bit of the mushroom marinade as the sauce. Garnish with the feta and serve.

Zoodle Taco Salad

zucchini noodles + spiced ground turkey + roasted chile guacamole + cherry tomatoes + chile citrus sauce

ORDER OF OPERATIONS
1. Prep the zucchini
2. Mash the guacamole
3. Make the sauce
4. Cook the turkey
5. Cook the zucchini
6. Assemble the bowls

zucchini noodles

2 large or 3 medium zucchini

1 Tbsp butter

1 Tbsp canola or vegetable oil

roasted chile guacamole

2 small-to-medium avocados, halved, pitted, and peeled

1 jalapeño or other hot green chile, roasted, peeled, seeded, and chopped, or about 1 Tbsp canned chopped green chile

1 garlic clove, minced

1 Tbsp fresh lime juice

Salt

chile citrus sauce

1 habanero chile, seeded and sliced (for less spice) or minced (for more spice)

2 Tbsp fresh lime juice

1 Tbsp fresh orange juice

¼ tsp salt

spiced ground turkey

1 Tbsp canola or vegetable oil

2 garlic cloves, minced

1 tsp ground cumin

¼ to ½ tsp cayenne pepper

1 lb [455 g] ground turkey

¼ tsp salt

⅓ cup [15 g] chopped fresh cilantro

Juice of ½ lime

12 cherry tomatoes, halved, for garnish

TO CUT THE ZUCCHINI NOODLES: Trim both ends off of each zucchini. One at a time, using a mandoline or a sharp knife, thinly each zucchini lengthwise, then cut the slices into long, narrow noodle-like strips (or use a spiralizer, if you have one). Transfer the strips to a medium bowl, cover, and set aside until ready to serve.

FOR THE GUACAMOLE: In a medium bowl, combine the avocados, chile, garlic, and lime juice and mash with a fork until smooth (or a bit chunky, if you like your guacamole chunky). Season with the salt.

FOR THE SAUCE: In a small bowl, combine the chile, lime juice, orange juice, and salt and mix well.

CONT'D

FOR THE TURKEY: In a large frying pan over medium-high heat, warm the oil. Add the garlic and cook, stirring, until it sizzles and is fragrant, about 30 seconds. Add the cumin and cayenne and stir to combine. Add the turkey and salt and cook, stirring frequently and breaking the meat up as you go, until browned and cooked through, about 5 minutes. Stir in the cilantro and lime juice, remove from the heat, and keep warm.

TO COOK THE ZUCCHINI: In a large frying pan over medium heat, melt the butter. Add the oil and swirl the pan to combine with the butter. Add the zucchini and cook, tossing gently to coat evenly, until warmed through, about 3 minutes.

TO ASSEMBLE: Divide the zucchini among four bowls. Top with the turkey and then with the guacamole and cherry tomatoes and serve. Pass the sauce at the table for everyone to sprinkle on to taste.

If everyone at the table is extra hungry, you can bulk up this bowl by adding one 14½-oz [415-g] can black beans, drained and rinsed, or 1¾ cups [420 g] drained Drunken Black Beans (page 24).

Budapest Bowl

mushroom barley pilaf + paprika-braised chicken + dilled white beans +
sweet pepper slaw + sour cream + dill

ORDER OF OPERATIONS

1. Cook the chicken
2. Make the pilaf
3. Make the slaw
4. Heat the beans
5. Assemble the bowls

paprika-braised chicken

1 lb [455 g] boneless, skinless chicken thighs

2 Tbsp canola or vegetable oil

2 Tbsp butter

1 onion, thinly sliced

2 Tbsp mild Hungarian paprika

1 tsp hot paprika, or ½ tsp cayenne pepper

1 cup [240 ml] chicken, vegetable, or
mushroom broth

mushroom barley pilaf

8 oz [230 g] button or cremini mushrooms

2 Tbsp butter

1 small onion, finely chopped

½ tsp fine sea salt

1 cup [180 g] pearled barley, rinsed

3 cups [720 ml] chicken, vegetable, or
mushroom broth

sweet pepper slaw

3 bell peppers (a mix of red, orange,
and yellow is nice)

3 Tbsp canola or olive oil

1 Tbsp white wine vinegar

½ tsp salt

½ tsp freshly ground black pepper

dilled white beans

One 14½-oz [415-g] can white beans, rinsed and
drained, or 1¾ cups [420 g] drained home-
cooked white beans (page 22)

½ cup [20 g] chopped fresh dill

Freshly ground black pepper

½ cup [120 ml] sour cream

Chopped fresh dill for garnish

FOR THE CHICKEN: Preheat the oven to
375°F [190°C]. Pat the chicken dry. In a large
frying pan or sauté pan with a tight-fitting lid,
warm the oil over medium-high heat. Add the
chicken and cook, undisturbed, until it starts
to brown on the underside, 3 to 4 minutes.
Turn the pieces over and brown on the second
side, 3 to 4 minutes longer. Transfer the
chicken to a plate. Add the butter to the same
pan and melt over medium-high heat. Add
the onion and cook, stirring, until soft, about
3 minutes. Add the mild and hot paprika and
cook, stirring, to coat the onion. Pour in the
broth and bring to a boil.

CONT'D

Return the chicken to the pan, cover, and transfer to the oven. Bake the chicken until it is very tender, about 30 minutes. Remove from the oven, uncover, and use a wooden spoon to separate the chicken into shreds (that's how tender it should be). Place the pan on the stove top over medium heat and cook, uncovered, until the sauce is reduced by one-third, about 20 minutes.

FOR THE PILAF: Begin the pilaf while the chicken is in the oven. Trim off the stem ends from the mushrooms, then cut off the stems. Finely chop the stems and thinly slice the caps. In a large saucepan over medium-high heat, melt the butter. Add the onion and salt and cook, stirring frequently, until the onion is soft, about 3 minutes. Increase the heat to high, add the mushroom stems and caps, and cook, stirring frequently, until the mushrooms release their liquid, about 5 minutes.

Add the barley and stir to mix everything well. Pour in the broth and stir again to mix. Bring to a boil, then lower the heat to maintain a steady simmer, cover partially, and cook, stirring every few minutes, until the liquid is absorbed and the barley is tender, about 30 minutes. If the liquid is absorbed before the barley is tender, add up to 1 cup [240 ml] water, ¼ cup [60 ml] at a time.

FOR THE SLAW: Seed and thinly slice the peppers. In a medium bowl, whisk together the oil, vinegar, salt, and pepper. Add the peppers and toss to combine.

FOR THE BEANS: In a medium saucepan over medium heat, warm the beans until hot (or put them in a microwave-safe bowl and heat them in the microwave). Add the dill, season with pepper, and toss to mix well.

TO ASSEMBLE: Divide the pilaf among four bowls. Arrange the chicken, beans, and slaw in three separate and equal sections on top of the pilaf. Dollop the sour cream on the chicken and sprinkle everything with the dill.

NOTE: Want to gild the comfort lily? Try this with Mashed Potatoes (page 46) instead of barley pilaf.

Tea Salad–Style Bowl (with Chicken!)

rice + mirin-braised chicken thighs + seared Brussels sprout leaf salad + sesame seeds + toasted peanuts + golden garlic + green onions

ORDER OF OPERATIONS

1. Marinate the chicken
2. Put the rice on to cook
3. Cook the chicken
4. Prep the salad
5. Ready the garnishes
6. Finish the salad
7. Assemble the bowls

mirin-braised chicken thighs

1 Tbsp soy sauce

1 Tbsp mirin

1 tsp freshly grated ginger

½ tsp red chile flakes

1½ lb [680 g] boneless, skinless chicken thighs, cut into bite-size pieces

1 cup short-grain or sweet brown rice

seared Brussels sprout leaf salad

1 lb [455 g] Brussels sprouts

1 garlic clove, minced

2-in [5-cm] piece fresh ginger, peeled and finely grated

1 serrano chile, minced

2 Tbsp fresh lime juice

1 Tbsp fish sauce

¼ tsp salt

garnishes

2 tsp sesame seeds

2 Tbsp raw peanuts

2 Tbsp canola, vegetable, or peanut oil

3 garlic cloves, thinly sliced

2 green onions, white and green parts, chopped

FOR THE CHICKEN: In a medium bowl, combine the soy sauce, mirin, ginger, and pepper flakes and mix well. Add the chicken, stir to coat evenly, cover, and let sit at room temperature for 30 to 60 minutes or refrigerate for up to overnight.

FOR THE RICE: Plan to put the rice on to cook about 1 hour before serving, following the directions for brown rice on page 15.

TO COOK THE CHICKEN: Heat a medium pot or a wok over medium heat. When the pot is hot, dump in the chicken and its marinade. When the mixture begins to simmer, turn the heat to medium-low or low to maintain a very gentle simmer. Cook, stirring every now and again, until the chicken is cooked through and very tender, about 35 minutes.

CONT'D

FOR THE SALAD: Peel off and discard any damaged leaves from the Brussels sprouts, then trim off the stems. Peel off as many layers of leaves from each sprout as you can until you reach the core, slice the core lengthwise as thinly as possible, and use both the leaves and sliced cores. (For quicker prep, just thinly slice the sprouts.)

To make the dressing for the salad, in a medium bowl, stir together the garlic, ginger, chile, lime juice, and fish sauce. Set the sprouts and dressing aside separately.

FOR THE GARNISHES: Heat a large cast-iron pan over medium-high heat. Add the sesame seeds and cook, stirring, until toasted, 1 to 2 minutes. Transfer to a plate or bowl.

Add the peanuts to the same pan and cook, stirring frequently, until toasted, about 3 minutes. Pour the nuts onto a cutting bowl, let cool, and finely chop.

Line a plate with a few layers of paper towels. Return the same pan to medium-high heat and add the oil. When the oil is hot, add the garlic and cook, stirring constantly, until golden, about 30 seconds. Using a slotted spoon, transfer the garlic to the towel-lined plate to drain. Pour the oil into a heatproof bowl and let cool.

TO FINISH THE SALAD: When the oil has cooled, pour it into the bowl holding the dressing and whisk to mix well. Without wiping out the pan used for the garnishes, return the pan to high heat. Add the leaves and sliced cores of the Brussels sprouts, or the sliced Brussels sprouts, and sprinkle with the salt. Cook, stirring now and again, until tender and any loose leaves have wilted to one-third of their original volume and are browned at the edges, 10 to 15 minutes.

Transfer the sprouts to the bowl holding the dressing and toss well. Let cool until just warm.

TO ASSEMBLE: Divide the rice among four bowls. Top half of the rice with the chicken and the other half with the Brussels sprouts. Sprinkle everything with the sesame seeds, peanuts, garlic, and green onions and serve.

Slurpy Soba Pork Bowl

soba noodles + soupy braised pork + poached egg +
pickled turnips with their greens

soupy braised pork

2-lb [910-g] piece boneless pork shoulder
or butt

½ tsp salt

1 Tbsp canola or vegetable oil

3 garlic cloves, crushed

1 large dried hot chile

One 12-fl oz [360-ml] bottle beer

pickled turnips with their greens

8 baby turnips with their greens

½ tsp salt

1 tsp rice vinegar

Pinch of sugar

1 tsp toasted sesame oil

½ tsp red pepper flakes (optional)

12 oz [340 g] dried soba noodles

4 eggs

FOR THE PORK: Sprinkle the pork all over
with the salt and let sit for at least 15 minutes
or cover and refrigerate for up to overnight.
Bring to room temperature before proceed-
ing. Preheat the oven to 350°F [180°C].

In a Dutch oven or other large, heavy pot over
medium-high heat, warm the oil. When the oil
is hot, add the pork and cook, undisturbed,
until well browned on the underside, 3 to
5 minutes. Turn the pork over and brown on
the second side, 3 to 5 minutes longer. Continue to turn the pork as needed to brown all
over. Add the garlic, chile, and beer and use
a wooden spoon to scrape up any browned
bits on the bottom of the pot. Cover, transfer
to the oven, and braise until the pork is very
tender, about 2 hours.

FOR THE TURNIPS: Cut the greens from the
turnips and set the greens aside. Trim the
turnips and cut each turnip into eight wedges.
Put the wedges in a bowl, sprinkle with the
salt, and let sit for 30 minutes. Pat the wedges
thoroughly dry (you can rinse them first if
you don't like things too salty), then rinse and
dry the bowl. Add the vinegar, sugar, sesame
oil, and the pepper flakes, if you want a spicy
version, to the bowl and whisk to mix well.
Add the turnips and toss to coat evenly. Let
sit for at least 30 minutes or up to overnight.
Cut the turnip greens into fine ribbons.

CONT'D

TO FINISH THE PORK: When the pork is ready, remove the pot from the oven. Transfer the pork to a cutting board or a platter and use two forks to pull it apart into shreds. Remove and discard the chile from the pot and mash the garlic into the cooking juices. Return the pork to the cooking juices and stir to coat evenly. Cover to keep warm.

FOR THE NOODLES AND EGGS: Cook the noodles as directed on page 19 and drain. At the same time, poach the eggs as directed on page 26.

TO ASSEMBLE: Divide the noodles among four bowls. Top with pork and its pan juices and then with a poached egg. Arrange some turnip wedges to one side of the egg and some turnip greens to the other side, then serve.

You cannot find baby turnips with their greens attached? Buy topped turnips and 1 bunch of any other fairly hearty green, like mustard or kale.

Minnesota Hotdish Bowl

wild rice black lentil pilaf + sausage + creamy mushroom sauce + garlicky chard + toasted walnuts

ORDER OF OPERATIONS

1. Cook the wild rice
2. Cook the sausage
3. Make the mushroom sauce
4. Cook the chard
5. Toast the walnuts
6. Assemble the bowls

wild rice black lentil pilaf

1 cup [180 g] wild rice

4 cups [960 ml] water or chicken or vegetable broth

1 tsp salt (if using water)

½ cup [80 g] black lentils

2 garlic sausages

creamy mushroom sauce

2 Tbsp butter

1 small onion, finely chopped

½ tsp salt

2 garlic cloves, minced

1 lb [455 g] button or cremini mushrooms, trimmed and sliced

1 cup [240 ml] heavy cream

Leaves from 3 fresh thyme sprigs

Freshly ground black pepper

garlicky chard

1 bunch Swiss chard, about 10 oz [280 g]

1 Tbsp butter

1 garlic clove, sliced

Salt

½ cup [65 g] walnut pieces

FOR THE WILD RICE: Put the wild rice and the water or broth in a pot; if using water, add the salt. Bring to a boil over high heat. Add the lentils and bring back to a boil. Cover, lower the heat to maintain a steady simmer, and cook until the wild rice and the lentils are tender, about 45 minutes. Uncover and cook, stirring, to cook off any excess liquid.

FOR THE SAUSAGES: In a large frying pan over medium heat, cook the sausages, turning as needed, until browned and cooked through, 4 to 5 minutes per side. Transfer to a plate and cover with aluminum foil. Don't wash the pan!

CONT'D

FOR THE MUSHROOM SAUCE: Return the pan you used for the sausages to medium heat and add the butter. When the butter melts, add the onion and salt and cook, stirring and scraping up any browned bits from the pan bottom as you go, until the onion is soft, about 3 minutes. Add the garlic and mushrooms and cook, stirring frequently, until the liquid the mushrooms release evaporates and the mushrooms begin to brown, about 10 minutes. Add the cream and thyme and simmer until thickened, about 5 minutes. Season with pepper and with more salt if needed. Remove from the heat and cover to keep warm.

FOR THE CHARD: Cut the stems off of the chard leaves. Chop the stems and the leaves, keeping them separate. In a large saucepan over medium-high heat, melt the butter. Add the garlic and chard stems, cover, and cook until the stems have softened, about 3 minutes. Add the leaves, stir to combine, and cook, stirring frequently, until the leaves and stems are tender, 3 to 5 minutes. Season with salt.

FOR THE WALNUTS: In a small frying pan over medium-high heat, toast the walnuts, shaking the pan frequently, until they start to smell toasty and take on a bit of color, 3 to 5 minutes. Take care not to let them darken too much in the pan, as they will continue to toast when you take them off the heat. Pour into a small bowl.

TO ASSEMBLE: Divide the wild rice among four bowls. Cut the sausages into bite-size slices and divide evenly among the bowls. Pour the mushroom sauce over the sausage and wild rice. Top with the chard and then the walnuts and serve.

Sizzling Beef Bowl

sesame brown rice + sizzling beef + charred vegetables + watercress + pepper lime sauce

ORDER OF OPERATIONS

1. Marinate the beef
2. Cook the rice
3. Prep the vegetables
4. Make the sauce
5. Cook the vegetables
6. Cook the beef
7. Assemble the bowls

sizzling beef

1 to 1½ lb [455 to 680 g] beef tenderloin or sirloin, cut into 1-in [2.5-cm] cubes

4 garlic cloves, chopped

2 Tbsp sugar

1 tsp salt

1 tsp freshly ground black pepper

¼ cup [60 ml] rice wine or white wine

3 Tbsp soy sauce

1 Tbsp fish sauce

2 Tbsp canola oil

1 Tbsp unsalted butter

sesame brown rice

3 cups [720 g] water

1 cup [200 g] sweet brown rice

¼ tsp salt

1 Tbsp sesame seeds

pepper lime sauce

2 limes

¼ tsp salt

¼ tsp freshly ground black pepper

charred vegetables

1 Tbsp canola oil

1 Tbsp butter

2 zucchini, trimmed, halved lengthwise, and cut crosswise into 1-in [2.5-cm] pieces

2 handfuls of green beans, about 8 oz [230 g], trimmed and cut into 2-in [5-cm] pieces

2 green onions, white and green parts, cut into 2-in [5-cm] pieces

½ tsp fine sea salt

2 cups [55 g] watercress leaves

TO MARINATE THE BEEF: Put the meat in a medium bowl. Sprinkle with the garlic, 1 Tbsp of the sugar, the salt, and the pepper and toss to coat evenly. Cover and let sit for about 30 minutes at room temperature or refrigerate for up to 1 day.

In a small bowl, whisk together the wine, soy sauce, fish sauce, and the remaining 1 Tbsp sugar and set aside until ready to cook.

CONT'D

FOR THE RICE: In a medium saucepan over high heat, combine the water, rice, and salt. Bring to a boil, stir, cover, turn the heat to low, and cook, undisturbed, for 45 minutes. Remove from the heat—leave the lid on!—and let sit for 10 to 15 minutes. The grains will be tender and the liquid will be absorbed.

While the rice is cooking, in a small frying pan over medium heat, toast the sesame seeds, shaking the pan frequently, until fragrant and just turning golden, 1 to 2 minutes. Remove from the heat and pour into a small bowl. When the rice is ready, uncover, fluff with a fork, and gently stir in the sesame seeds. Cover to keep warm while you prepare the remaining components.

FOR THE SAUCE: Halve the limes and juice the halves into a small bowl. Whisk in the salt and pepper.

FOR THE VEGETABLES: In a large frying pan over high heat, warm together the canola oil and butter. When the butter is melted, add the zucchini, green beans, and green onions, spreading them in a single layer as much as possible. Sprinkle with the salt. Cook, undisturbed, until well browned on the underside, about 3 minutes. Turn the vegetables and brown on the second side, about 3 minutes longer. Remove from the heat and cover to keep warm.

TO COOK THE BEEF: Heat a wok or other a large, heavy sauté pan over high heat. When the pan is hot, add the oil. When the oil shimmers, swirl the pan to coat with the oil, then add the beef in a single layer. Cook the beef, undisturbed, until well browned on the underside, about 4 minutes. Turn the pieces and cook until browned on the second side, about 4 minutes longer. Using a slotted spoon, transfer the beef to a medium bowl.

Return the pan to medium-high heat, add the wine mixture, and use a wooden spoon to scrape up any browned bits from the pan bottom. Simmer until the liquid is reduced by one-third, just a few minutes. Add the butter, shaking the pan until the butter melts and incorporates with the sauce, and then add the beef and any accumulated juices back into the pan. Stir to coat the beef with the sauce. Remove from the heat.

TO ASSEMBLE: Divide the rice among four bowls. Arrange the beef on one side of the rice and the vegetables on the other side. Spoon the beef pan sauce over the beef. Strew the watercress evenly over the top and serve. Pass the lime sauce at the table for diners to drizzle on their bowls as they like.

Reuben Bowl

caraway rye pilaf + pastrami + sauerkraut + pickle + Swiss cheese + Russian dressing

ORDER OF OPERATIONS

1. Make the pilaf
2. Make the dressing
3. Prep the sauerkraut
4. Prep toppings
5. Chop and heat the pastrami
6. Assemble the bowls

caraway rye pilaf

1 Tbsp canola or vegetable oil

1 onion, finely chopped

½ tsp salt

1 tsp caraway seeds

1 cup [200 g] rye kernels

3 cups [720 ml] chicken or vegetable broth

½ tsp freshly ground black pepper

Russian dressing

½ cup [115 g] mayonnaise

2 Tbsp ketchup

2 tsp prepared horseradish

½ to 1 tsp hot sauce

½ tsp Worcestershire sauce

¼ tsp mild paprika

1 cup [150 g] drained sauerkraut

2 medium-size dill pickles, chopped

½ cup [55 g] shredded Swiss cheese

8 oz [230 g] pastrami, chopped

FOR THE PILAF: In a large frying pan over medium-high heat, warm the oil. Add the onion and salt and cook, stirring occasionally, until the onion is soft, about 3 minutes. Add the caraway seeds and cook, stirring frequently, until the caraway smells toasted, about 2 minutes. Add the rye kernels and stir to combine. Pour in the broth, bring to a boil, cover, turn the heat to low, and cook until the kernels are tender to the bite, about 45 minutes. Stir in the pepper and remove from the heat. Cover to keep warm.

FOR THE DRESSING: In a small bowl, combine the mayonnaise, ketchup, horseradish, hot sauce to taste, Worcestershire sauce, and paprika and stir to mix well.

FOR THE SAUERKRAUT: Using your hands (or wrap the sauerkraut in a clean kitchen towel), squeeze out as much excess moisture from the sauerkraut as possible.

FOR THE PASTRAMI: Put the pastrami in a small frying pan, cover, place over medium-low heat, and heat, uncovering to stir once or twice, until hot, 2 to 3 minutes.

CONT'D

TO ASSEMBLE: Divide the pilaf among four bowls. Top with the pastrami, pile on the sauerkraut, and sprinkle on the pickles. Drizzle with the dressing, strew with the cheese, and serve.

MAKE IT EASY: Rye kernels can be tricky to track down. Barley or farro is a tasty substitute here. See pages 15 and 17, respectively, for the timing for these grains. Also, if you are really pressed for time, use bottled Russian dressing.

Rice-Free Korean Grill

ribboned kale + Korean-spiced steak + kimchi-style Brussels sprouts + roasted red onion + watermelon radishes + sesame seeds

ORDER OF OPERATIONS

1. Make the Brussels sprouts
2. Roast the onions
3. Prep the steak
4. Cook the steak
5. Prep the kale
6. Slice the radishes
7. Assemble the bowls

kimchi-style Brussels sprouts

1 lb [455 g] Brussels sprouts

1½ tsp salt

1 small garlic clove, minced

1 Tbsp *gochugaru* (Korean red chile flakes)

2 to 3 tsp sugar

1 tsp rice vinegar

1 tsp toasted sesame oil

roasted red onions

2 small red onions

1 Tbsp canola or vegetable oil

Korean-spiced steak

1 garlic clove, minced

1 Tbsp *gochugaru* (Korean red chile flakes)

1 Tbsp toasted sesame oil

1 Tbsp soy sauce

1 Tbsp mirin

1½ to 2 lb [680 to 910 g] chateaubriand steak, trimmed of excess fat

2 tsp canola, cold-pressed sesame, or vegetable oil

ribboned kale

1 bunch Tuscan kale

¼ tsp canola or cold-pressed sesame oil

¼ tsp salt

1 large watermelon radish, peeled and thinly sliced

2 tsp sesame seeds, toasted

FOR THE BRUSSELS SPROUTS: Peel off the darker green outer leaves from the Brussels sprouts, then trim off the stems. Cut the sprouts lengthwise into halves or quarters. Put the pieces into a colander set over a large bowl, sprinkle with the salt, and toss gently to combine. Let sit for at least 1 hour or up to several hours. (The salt will draw water out of the sprouts. It won't be a huge amount, given their dense texture, but it will be some, which will soften them a bit.)

CONT'D

Lay the sprouts on a clean kitchen towel or on layers of paper towels and roll up tightly to squeeze out even more water. Transfer the sprouts to a medium bowl, add the garlic, *gochugaru*, sugar (use the larger amount if you generally like a little more sweetness), rice vinegar, and toasted sesame oil, and toss to mix thoroughly. Cover and refrigerate for at least 1 hour or up to 1 week.

FOR THE ONIONS: Preheat the oven to 450°F [230°C]. Peel the onions and cut each onion into eight wedges. Oil a baking pan that will accommodate the onion wedges without crowding them. Set the wedges in the pan and turn them until they are coated on all sides with oil. Roast until browned on the edges and tender, about 20 minutes. Remove from the oven and let sit until ready to use.

FOR THE STEAK: In a baking pan large enough to hold the steak, combine the garlic, *gochugaru*, toasted sesame oil, soy sauce, and mirin. Add the steak, turning it to coat with the marinade. Let sit for at least 10 minutes or up to 30 minutes.

The steak can be cooked on the stove top, under the broiler, or on a grill. To panfry: Preheat a large cast-iron frying pan or other heavy frying pan over high heat and add the canola oil. When the oil shimmers, swirl the pan to coat it with the oil, then add the steak, with the marinade clinging to it. It should sizzle immediately. Cook until a brown crust forms on the underside, about 5 minutes. Flip the steak and cook until browned on the second side, about 5 minutes longer, for rare. If you like your steak done medium-rare, cook for 6 minutes on each side; for medium, 7 minutes on each side; for well-done go toward 8 to 9 minutes on each side.

TO BROIL: Set an oven rack about 3 in [7.5 cm] from the heating element and preheat the broiler. Set the steak, with the marinade clinging to it, on a baking sheet or broiler pan and slip under the broiler. Cook, turning it once, until browned on both sides, about 5 minutes on each side for rare. If you like your steak done medium-rare, cook for 6 minutes on each side; for medium, 7 minutes on each side; for well-done go toward 8 to 9 minutes on each side.

TO GRILL: Prepare a fire in a charcoal or gas grill for direct-heat cooking over high heat. (You should be able to hold your hand about 1 in [2.5 cm] above the cooking grate for 1 to 2 seconds before you must pull it away.) Oil the cooking grate. Set the steak on the grate directly over the fire and cook, turning it once, until grill marks form on both sides, 5 minutes for rare. If you like your steak done medium-rare, cook for 6 minutes on each side; for medium, 7 minutes on each side; for well-done go toward 8 to 9 minutes on each side.

Let the steak rest for at least 10 minutes and up to 20 minutes before cutting it against the grain into slices for adding to the bowls.

FOR THE KALE: While the steak rests, trim the thick stems from the kale and cut the leaves into ribbons as finely as possible. Put the ribbons in a large bowl, drizzle with the oil, and toss to coat evenly. Sprinkle with the salt and toss again. Use your hands to squeeze and massage the kale by the handful to soften it. It should reduce in volume by about one-half.

TO ASSEMBLE: Divide the kale among four bowls. Top with the steak slices and drizzle on any accumulated steak juices. Arrange the Brussels sprouts and roasted onions to either side of the steak. Garnish with the radish slices, sprinkle the entire surface with the sesame seeds, and serve.

MAKE IT EASY: Use store-bought kimchi instead of the Brussels sprouts and raw onion slices instead of the roasted wedges.

Better-than-a-Kebab

lemony freekeh + minted meatballs + chopped cucumber salad + baked eggplant +
sumac + cherry tomatoes + white garlic sauce

ORDER OF OPERATIONS
1. Brine the eggplant
2. Make the sauce
3. Bake the eggplant
4. Cook the freekeh
5. Prep the meatballs
6. Make the salad
7. Cook the meatballs
8. Assemble the bowls

baked eggplant

4 cups [960 ml] water

1 Tbsp salt

1 globe eggplant, trimmed and sliced crosswise

white garlic sauce

1 head garlic

1 Tbsp fresh lemon juice

1 tsp salt

1 cup [240 ml] canola oil

lemony freekeh

1 cup [180 g] freekeh

2 cups [480 ml] chicken or vegetable broth

1 Tbsp fresh lemon juice

1 tsp finely grated lemon zest

minted meatballs

1½ lb [680 g] ground meat (lamb is lovely here,
but beef or turkey will work, too)

1 small onion

4 garlic cloves, minced

½ cup [15 g] fresh mint leaves, minced

2 Tbsp mild paprika

2 tsp ground cumin

¾ tsp salt

¼ tsp cayenne pepper (optional)

1 to 2 Tbsp canola or vegetable oil

chopped cucumber salad

1 large English or other slicing cucumber, peeled,
halved lengthwise, seeded, and chopped

1 tsp minced fresh mint

1 tsp rice vinegar

1 tsp extra-virgin olive oil

Salt

1 tsp ground sumac

1 cup [150 g] grape or cherry tomatoes, halved

CONT'D

TO BRINE THE EGGPLANT: Pour the water into a bowl large enough to accommodate the eggplant slices. Add the salt and stir to dissolve. Put the eggplant slices in the salted water and top the eggplant with a plate slightly smaller than the diameter of the bowl to keep them submerged. Let sit for about 30 minutes. Meanwhile, preheat the oven to 400°F [200°C]. Spray a baking sheet with olive oil cooking spray.

FOR THE SAUCE: Separate the head of garlic into cloves and peel the cloves. If you want to tame the sharp garlic flavor of this sauce, bring a small saucepan filled with water to a boil over high heat, add the garlic cloves, blanch for 1 minute, drain, and proceed with the recipe. If you prefer to keep the flavor intense, skip this step and use raw garlic (I do!). In a blender, combine the garlic, lemon juice, and salt and whirl until more or less smooth. With the blender running on medium speed, add the canola oil in a very slow, steady stream. The oil will blend with the garlic mixture, resulting in an almost-fluffy and brilliantly white sauce. Cover and set aside. Garlic lovers will want to dollop this sauce on at will, but they need to make sure that anyone they kiss later has eaten it, too.

TO BAKE THE EGGPLANT: Drain the eggplant slices and pat them thoroughly dry. Set the eggplant slices on the prepared pan in a single layer and spray the tops with cooking spray. Bake the slices, turning them once after 15 minutes, until browned on both sides and tender, about 30 minutes total. If the slices fail to brown but are tender, turn on the broiler, position the oven rack about 3 in [7.5 cm] from the heating element, and broil the slices on both sides until browned. Remove from the oven, let cool, and cut into narrow strips. Set aside.

FOR THE FREEKEH: Heat a medium, heavy saucepan over medium-high heat. When the pan is hot, add the freekeh and cook, stirring or shaking the pan often, until the freekeh is toasted and fragrant, about 3 minutes. Add the broth and bring to a boil. Cover, turn the heat to low, and cook, undisturbed, until the liquid is absorbed and the freekeh is tender, 20 to 25 minutes. Remove from the heat, uncover, fluff with a fork, and stir in the lemon juice and zest. Re-cover and let sit until serving, then fluff again just before serving.

TO PREP THE MEATBALLS: In a large bowl, break up the ground meat into small pieces. Using the large holes of a box grater, grate the onion onto the meat. Sprinkle the garlic, mint, paprika, cumin, salt, and cayenne (if using) over the meat and onion, then, using your fingers, gently mix everything together.

Divide the mixture into twelve equal portions. Roll each portion into a ball between your palms and place on a platter or baking sheet. (Dampening your hands with water will help keep the meat from sticking to them.) Set aside while you make the salad.

FOR THE SALAD: In a medium bowl, combine the cucumber, mint, vinegar, and olive oil and toss to mix well. Season with salt and mix again.

TO COOK THE MEATBALLS: Heat a large frying pan over medium-high heat. Add 1 Tbsp of the oil to the pan and swirl the pan to coat the bottom evenly. Add the meatballs and cook, turning them as needed and adding a little more oil if necessary to prevent sticking, until browned all over and cooked through, about 8 minutes total.

TO ASSEMBLE: Divide the freekeh among four bowls. Arrange three meatballs on the center of the freekeh in each bowl. Put the cucumber salad and the eggplant on either side of the meatballs. Sprinkle the sumac over everything, finish with the tomatoes, and serve. Pass the garlic sauce at the table.

Bulgur (page 16) works equally well as a base, as would a bed of raw or sautéed shredded greens. If the garlic sauce sounds too intense, try Herbed Yogurt Sauce (page 146) instead.

full bowls

145

Cauliflower Couscous Bowl

spiced cauliflower "couscous" + garam masala lamb patties + garlic-braised artichokes + spinach + tomatillo chile relish + herbed yogurt sauce

ORDER OF OPERATIONS
1. Cook the artichokes
2. Make the sauce
3. Make the relish
4. Cook the cauliflower
5. Cook the lamb
6. Assemble the bowls

garlic-braised artichokes

½ cup [120 ml] fresh lemon juice

4 artichokes

1 cup [240 ml] water

¼ cup [60 ml] extra-virgin olive oil

½ tsp salt

2 garlic cloves, minced

Leaves from 6 fresh mint sprigs, minced

1 fresh thyme sprig

herbed yogurt sauce

½ cup [120 ml] plain whole-milk yogurt

1 garlic clove, minced

2 Tbsp minced fresh cilantro

1 Tbsp minced fresh mint

¼ tsp salt

1 tsp olive oil

½ tsp fresh lemon juice

tomatillo chile relish

2 tomatillos, husks removed and rinsed

1 jalapeño chile

1 garlic clove

¼ tsp salt

spiced cauliflower "couscous"

1 head cauliflower

2 Tbsp butter

1 onion, finely chopped

½ tsp ground cumin

½ tsp ground coriander

¼ tsp ground turmeric

½ tsp ground ginger

garam masala lamb patties

1 lb [455 g] ground lamb

1 garlic clove, minced

2 tsp garam masala

½ tsp salt

½ tsp freshly ground black pepper

1 cup [30 g] baby spinach or arugula leaves

FOR THE ARTICHOKES: Fill a large bowl with water and add ¼ cup [60 ml] of the lemon juice. Working with one artichoke at a time, trim off the end of the stem and then pull off the outer leaves until you reach a solid 2-in [5-cm] cone of very light green (almost

CONT'D

yellow) leaves. Cut off the prickly deeper green tops of the leaves. Using a paring knife, trim off all of the dark and medium green areas around the base of the artichoke and the stem. Cut the trimmed artichoke lengthwise into quarters, scoop out the fuzzy choke from each quarter, and slip the quarters into the lemon water. Repeat with the remaining artichokes.

Put the remaining ¼ cup [60 ml] lemon juice in a saucepan large enough to hold all of the artichokes and add the water, olive oil, salt, garlic, mint, and thyme. Bring to a boil over high heat, add the artichokes, and adjust the heat to maintain a steady simmer. Cook the artichokes, stirring now and again, until they are tender when pierced with the tip of a knife, 20 to 30 minutes. Remove from the heat and cover to keep warm or let come to room temperature.

FOR THE SAUCE: In a medium bowl, combine the yogurt, garlic, cilantro, mint, salt, olive oil, and lemon juice and stir to mix well. Let sit for at least 10 minutes or up to 1 hour to allow the flavors to blend.

FOR THE RELISH: Mince the tomatillos, chile, and garlic (or pulse them in a food processor). Transfer to a bowl and stir in the salt. Set aside.

FOR THE CAULIFLOWER: Trim the cauliflower and break it into florets. Put the florets in a food processor and pulse until they break down into grain-like bits. (I have found the cauliflower breaks apart fairly quickly, but usually one or two pieces remain whole. I solve this by dumping the "couscous" into a

large bowl, pulling out the large pieces, and pulsing those until they break down, too.)

In a large frying pan over medium-high heat, melt the butter. Add the onion and cook, stirring frequently, until browned on the edges, about 5 minutes. Add the cumin, coriander, turmeric, and ginger and stir to combine. Add the cauliflower and cook, stirring frequently, until warmed through, about 5 minutes. Remove from the heat and cover to keep warm.

FOR THE LAMB: In a medium bowl, break up the lamb into small pieces. Sprinkle with the garlic, garam masala, salt, and pepper and, using your fingers, gently mix everything together. Divide into eight or twelve equal portions and pat each portion into a patty ½ inch [12 mm] thick.

Heat a large frying pan over medium-high heat. When the pan is hot, add the patties and cook, turning once, until browned on both sides and cooked through, about 4 minutes per side.

TO ASSEMBLE: Divide the cauliflower among four bowls. Arrange the lamb, artichokes, and spinach in three separate and equal sections on top of the cauliflower. Add dollops of the relish and the yogurt sauce and serve.

MAKE IT EASY: The artichokes are delicious, but the bowl is still perfectly tasty (and has tons of flavor) without them. A store-bought green salsa could easily stand in for the tomatillo relish.

Cardamom Lamb Bowl

browned garlic bulgur + roasted eggplant salad + shredded cardamom lamb + yogurt + pomegranate seeds

ORDER OF OPERATIONS
1. Cook the lamb
2. Cook the eggplant
3. Cook the bulgur
4. Make the eggplant salad
5. Assemble the bowls

shredded cardamom lamb

2 lamb shanks

½ tsp salt

½ tsp freshly ground black pepper

1 tsp vegetable oil

1 tsp Sichuan peppercorns (optional)

4 cardamom pods

3 garlic cloves

2 whole cloves

1 star anise pod

1 cup [240 ml] dry red wine

1 cup [240 ml] chicken or vegetable broth

1 Tbsp butter (optional)

roasted eggplant salad

1 medium eggplant

2 green onions, white and green parts, minced

1 garlic clove, minced

⅓ cup [7 g] fresh mint or cilantro leaves, chopped

1 Tbsp extra-virgin olive oil

1 Tbsp fresh lemon juice

Salt

browned garlic bulgur

1 cup [140 g] bulgur

¼ tsp salt

1½ cups [360 ml] boiling water

3 Tbsp butter

1 garlic clove, minced

½ tsp freshly ground black pepper

½ cup [120 ml] plain whole-milk yogurt

Seeds from 1 pomegranate

FOR THE LAMB: Preheat the oven to 375°F [190°C]. Sprinkle the lamb shanks all over with the salt and pepper. Select an ovenproof pot or frying pan with a tight-fitting lid that will accommodate the lamb shanks without crowding. Add the vegetable oil and warm over medium heat. Add the shanks and cook, turning them as needed, until browned all over, about 10 minutes. Add the Sichuan peppercorns (if using), cardamom, garlic, cloves, and star anise and pour in the wine. Cover, transfer to the oven, and cook until the lamb is extremely tender and pulling away from the bone, about 1¼ hours.

CONT'D

Remove from the oven and transfer the lamb shanks to a plate. Remove and discard the cardamom, cloves, star anise, and as many of the peppercorns as you can from the cooking juices. Mash the garlic into the cooking juices and then place the pot over medium-high heat. Whisk in the broth, adjust the heat to maintain a simmer, and cook, whisking now and again, until the sauce is reduced by half. Whisk in the butter, if using. Meanwhile, use a fork to pull the meat off the bones and pull it into shreds. When the sauce is reduced, add the meat, stir to combine, and keep warm.

FOR THE EGGPLANT SALAD: Put the eggplant on a baking sheet, place in the oven with the lamb, and roast until it starts to collapse, about 1 hour. Alternatively, place the eggplant over the flame of a gas burner on the stove top (line the burner with aluminum foil to make cleanup easier) and roast, turning it as needed to char on all sides, until it starts to collapse, about 20 minutes.

Transfer the eggplant to a bowl or rimmed plate (it will release juices as it cools) to cool slightly until it can be handled. Discard any accumulated juices, then peel the eggplant, transfer to a cutting board, and chop finely. Transfer to a medium bowl, add the green onions, garlic, mint, olive oil, and lemon juice and stir to mix. Season with salt.

FOR THE BULGUR: In a medium heatproof bowl, combine the bulgur and salt. Add the water, cover, and let sit until the bulgur is tender and the water is absorbed, about 20 minutes. (Sometimes a batch absorbs less liquid; if the bulgur is tender, drain off any excess water.)

When the bulgur is ready, in a small saucepan over medium heat, melt the butter. Once the butter has melted, continue heating it, swirling the pan, until it starts to brown. Add the garlic and cook, stirring, until the butter browns evenly and smells toasty but not burned and the garlic starts to turn golden, about 1 minute. Stir the garlic and butter and the pepper into the bulgur.

TO ASSEMBLE: Divide the bulgur among four bowls. Top with the eggplant salad and then with the lamb, spooning some of the sauce from the lamb over the entire bowl. Garnish with a dollop of the yogurt, sprinkle with the pomegranate seeds, and serve.

INDEX

bowls!

The degree to which I've always preferred to eat out of bowls wouldn't have struck me as a professional asset without Sarah Billingsley and the whole crew at Chronicle Books. I am tremendously grateful for what they've managed to make of my weird combinations and crack-pot ideas. A big thanks to Nicole Franzen and her team for making my food look as yummy as I think it tastes—I'm all apologies for making them work in such a restricted everything-chopped-up-in-a-bowl format. As always, Doe Coover provided invaluable guidance and support.

While Tara Duggan and I never got a completely different book off the ground, many of the flavors here were first explored with her, and I have great faith that our united vision of cooking for modern families will prevail. She and her family (I'm looking at you Eric, Dahlia, and Elsie Gustafson) provided much needed early tasting support that buoyed my spirits at a key juncture.

A range of other friends, family, and colleagues have served as taste-testers and otherwise directly supported this book. The list includes Elissa Auther, Jordanna Bailkin, Bruce Cole, Marianne Condrup, Leah Donnelly, Julianne Gilland, Juliet Glass, Amy Machnak Hash, Amanda Hughen, Clare Leschin-Hoar, Adam O'Connor, Michelle Ohlmeyer, Marc Rasic, Jess Vacek, Kate Washington, and Watsons and Wolfs with all sorts of first names. Mary and Steve Watson, Mary Ann Wolf, and Nancy and Denny Watson, were, as always, extra enthusiastic.

My best tasters came in the form of Steven and Ernest Wolf. Two more honest yet loving critics are not to be found. Their humor and flexibility (and shopping and clean-up help) made it a pleasure to cook and serve everything found in these pages. Thanks to Ernest, we also know that all said food can be served on a plate to equally delicious effect.

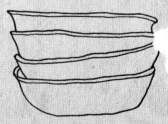